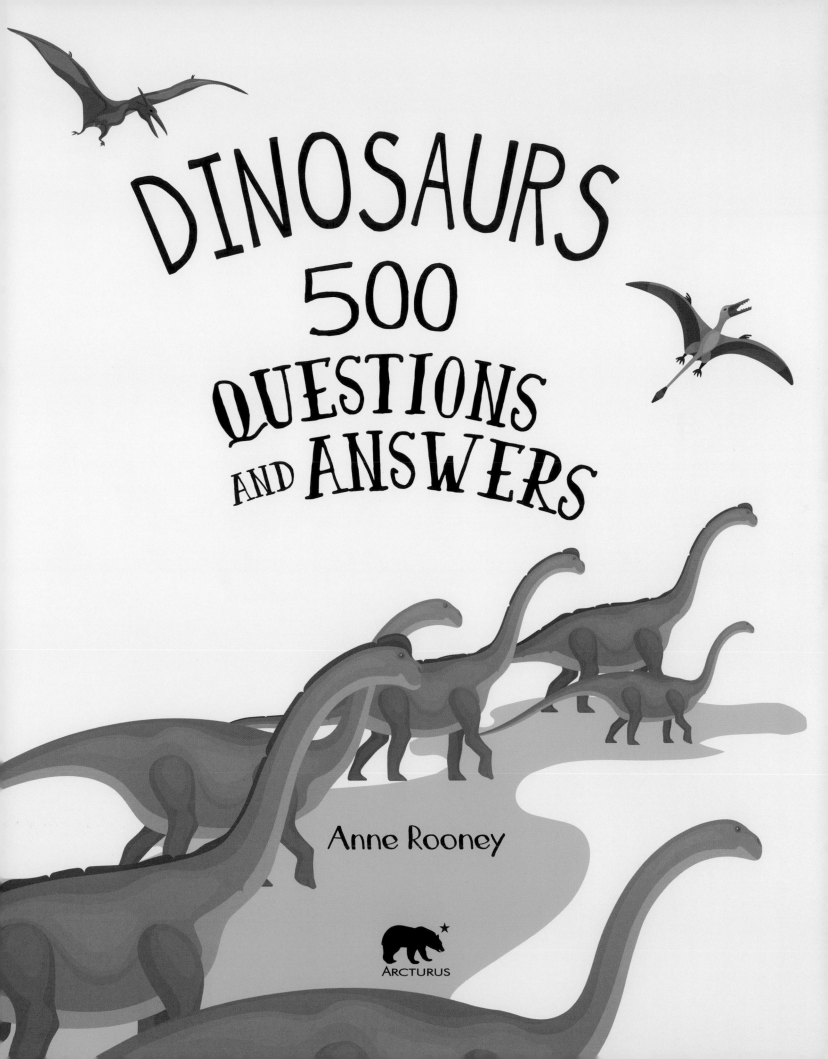

DINOSAURS
500
QUESTIONS AND ANSWERS

Anne Rooney

ARCTURUS

ARCTURUS

This edition published in 2022 by Arcturus Publishing Limited
26/27 Bickels Yard, 151–153 Bermondsey Street,
London SE1 3HA

Author: Anne Rooney
Editors: William Potter and Violet Peto
Designer: Sarah Fountain
Illustrator: Jake McDonald
Supplementary Artworks: Shutterstock
Design Manager: Jessica Holliland
Editorial Manager: Joe Harris

ISBN: 978-1-3988-1462-2
CH008650NT
Supplier 29, Date 0222, Print run 11803

Printed in China

INTRODUCTION

If you had a chance to ask a dinosaur expert any question, what would you ask?

Could I outrun a T. rex?

What was the biggest dinosaur?

What can you learn from dino poop?

How did the dinosaurs die out?

Are birds dinosaurs?

In this book, you'll find the answers to hundreds of clever questions like these. Then, turn to page 96 to learn how to get your tongue around all those long, tricky dinosaur names.

And guess what!? Once you've made it to the last page, you'll be able to claim you're a dinosaur expert, too!

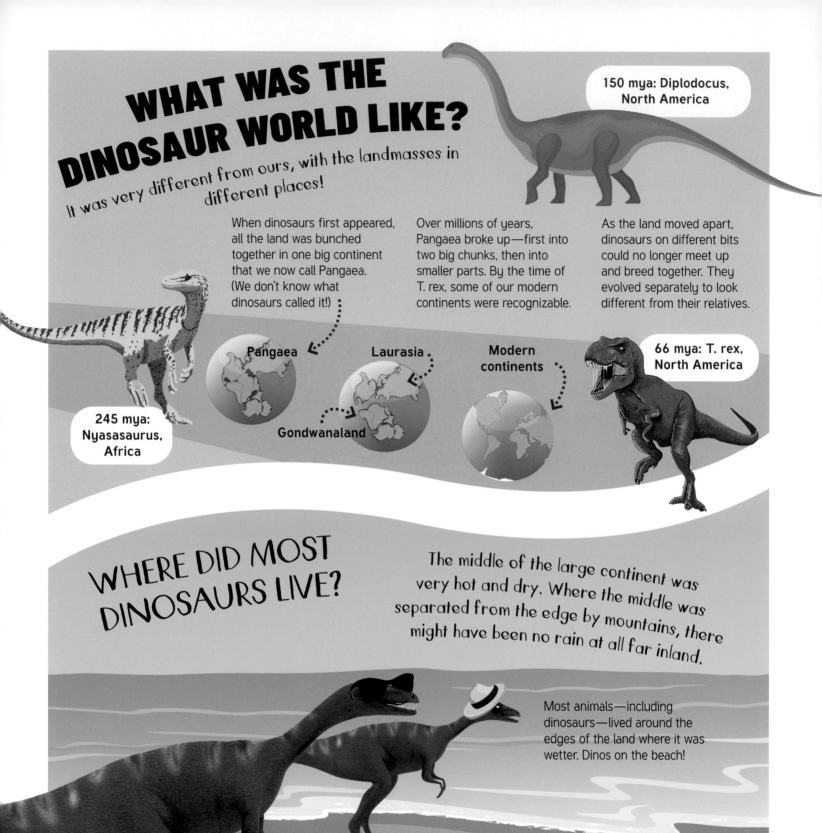

WHAT WAS THE DINOSAUR WORLD LIKE?

It was very different from ours, with the landmasses in different places!

150 mya: Diplodocus, North America

When dinosaurs first appeared, all the land was bunched together in one big continent that we now call Pangaea. (We don't know what dinosaurs called it!)

Over millions of years, Pangaea broke up—first into two big chunks, then into smaller parts. By the time of T. rex, some of our modern continents were recognizable.

As the land moved apart, dinosaurs on different bits could no longer meet up and breed together. They evolved separately to look different from their relatives.

Pangaea

Laurasia

Modern continents

Gondwanaland

66 mya: T. rex, North America

245 mya: Nyasasaurus, Africa

WHERE DID MOST DINOSAURS LIVE?

The middle of the large continent was very hot and dry. Where the middle was separated from the edge by mountains, there might have been no rain at all far inland.

Most animals—including dinosaurs—lived around the edges of the land where it was wetter. Dinos on the beach!

Was there only one ocean?
When there was just one big continent, that meant there was also one really big ocean, which we call the Tethys Ocean. It held seagoing reptiles, giant squid-like animals that lived in shells, fish, and sharks.

HOW TOASTY WAS IT IN THE DINOSAUR WORLD?

We worry about climate change now, but the world was much hotter in the days of the dinosaurs—we wouldn't survive.

Herrerasaurus

Anyone seen my sunscreen?

What was the temperature?
In the Triassic, when the first dinosaurs were around, the average global temperature was 30°C (86°F). It was even hotter in the water.

Was the sea hotter, too?
The temperature of the sea was 40°C (104°F), which would feel like a nice, warm bath. It was the hottest the temperature had been in hundreds of millions of years.

How does that compare with today?
Today, the average air temperature is a chilly 14°C (57°F) and the oceans 16°C (61°F).

WHAT WAS THE WEATHER LIKE FOR DINOS?

Was it always sunny?
All the pictures you ever see of dinosaurs show them in nice sunny weather. But they didn't enjoy 165 million years of sunshine. Although it was generally warmer than it is now, dinosaurs still had to face wind, rain, fog, and hail.

Please can someone invent an umbrella?

How did dinosaurs keep warm and dry?
Many dinosaurs had feathers, or something like feathers, which could have helped to keep them warm. Others had hard or scaly skin, which rain would have run off. But it probably wasn't nice. A giant sauropod like Diplodocus couldn't hide in a cave or a burrow. It had to just stand there, in the wind, rain, fog, or sunshine.

WERE ALL DINOSAURS JURASSIC?

Everyone has heard of Jurassic World, and the word "Jurassic" is always linked with dinosaurs. But there were lots of non-Jurassic dinosaurs, too.

What were the dinosaur ages?
Geologists split Earth's history into different ages. Dinosaurs lived in three of those ages—the Triassic, the Jurassic, and the Cretaceous.

TRIASSIC

Herrerasaurus

When did dinosaurs first appear?
The first true dinosaurs appeared in the early Triassic. They were fairly small and quick, and shared the world with lots of other animals.

JURASSIC

In the Jurassic, dinosaurs really took over. There were loads, and some of them were extremely big.

Diplodocus

Stegosaurus

CRETACEOUS

T. rex

Triceratops

The Cretaceous was also a great time for dinosaurs— or it was until things went badly wrong at the end. (See page 17.)

WERE DINOSAURS REPTILES?

Yes. The first reptiles appeared about 320 million years ago and evolved over time into different types.

What are today's reptiles like?
Reptiles living today include crocodiles, tortoises, and snakes.

I'm thoroughly modern you know.

You mean thoroughly scary!

Did crocodiles and snakes live with dinosaurs?
Crocodilians (animals like crocodiles) and snakes both evolved during the time of the dinosaurs. But they weren't like modern crocodiles and snakes. Early crocodiles lived mostly on land, but then they moved into swamps and rivers. Early snakes evolved from lizards that had legs and possibly lived in burrows.

DID DINOSAURS REACH ANTARCTICA?

Yes. Until 85 million years ago, Australia and Antarctica were joined with just a valley between them.

Leaellynasaura

Isn't Antarctica too cold for dinos?
Now, Antarctica is horribly cold, covered with a vast ice sheet all year round, and has no trees. In the time of the dinosaurs, it was warmer, and the valley might have been a lush forest. Australia has drifted north and become hotter.

Which dinosaurs lived there?
Dinosaurs found as fossils in the valley could move between the two easily. They include Diluvicursor, about the size of a turkey, and Leaellynasaura, a small plant-eater with a long tail.

Diluvicursor

WAS NORTH AMERICA LIKE IT IS NOW?

No. A hundred million years ago, the land that's now North America was split in two by a sea, which we call the Western Interior Seaway.

What was early North America like?
On one side, the west coast was a giant island stretching from Alaska to California. On the other, the Hudson Sea split the east and the middle from most of Canada.

Hardly any dinosaurs have been found in the east—just a few bones.

Did T. rex live all across North America?
Dinosaurs couldn't cross the sea so they developed differently on each chunk of land. That's why T. rex and Triceratops are found only in the west of the USA.

HOW WET WAS EUROPE?

In the Cretaceous period, sea levels were higher than now, and much of Europe was covered by sea.

Zalmoxes, Romania

Telmatosaurus, Romania

Did dinosaurs get marooned?
There were just islands sticking up above the waves. Dinosaurs were stranded on them as sea levels rose.

Magyarosaurus, Hungary

Why are Romanian dinos special?
One of the islands, called Haţeg, was about 200 km (125 miles) from any other land—too far for dinosaurs to swim to. It's now in Romania. The area has its own unique dinosaur fossils because the dinosaurs there evolved on their own, cut off from others.

Haţeg Island

ARE THERE SEA FOSSILS IN KANSAS?

Kansas is right in the middle of the USA, but it has fossils of plesiosaurs that lived in the Cretaceous sea.

Ammonite fossils

How did the beach reach a mountaintop?
As the landmasses have moved around, some chunks of land that were once at the coast have ended up in the middle of continents and even at the tops of mountains.

Plesiosaur

How are mountains made?
The Earth's surface is made of big slabs of land that move slowly around. When two collide, they join. The edges sometimes push upward, making mountains. The edges were originally the coast, and carry the fossils of sea creatures with them.

HOW WAS THE AIR DIFFERENT TO NOW?

Dinosaurs lived in an atmosphere of only 10-15 percent oxygen, while today's air is 21 percent oxygen.

Plateosaurus

Stegosaurus

So many yummy plants!

Was there more carbon dioxide, too?
Yes. More carbon dioxide (CO_2) leads to higher temperatures—that's why rising carbon dioxide levels are linked with global warming today. But dinosaurs didn't mind. They evolved to live at higher temperatures, with less oxygen and more carbon dioxide around them.

Why was more CO_2 better for some dinosaurs?
Plants need carbon dioxide, so high levels meant that there were lots of plants to eat and forests to hide in.

DID DINOSAURS RULE THE EARTH?

Although the first dinosaurs appeared in the early Triassic, they didn't immediately take over.

Who was in charge?
The world wasn't quite ready for dinosaurs. It was too hot for them to spread everywhere. Other groups of archosaurs (which means "ruling reptiles") were in charge.

Postosuchus

Lystrosaurus

Euparkeria

What happened to the archosaurs?
Around 199 million years ago, disaster struck. Most archosaurs were wiped out by a catastrophe of some kind, and the dinosaurs rose in their place.

What kind of catastrophe?
No one is quite sure what happened. One idea is that massive volcanic eruptions changed the atmosphere and climate. A period when lots of species die off is called a mass extinction event.

DID ALL DINOSAURS BECOME EXTINCT?

No. The types of dinosaurs that became extinct 66 million years ago are called "non-avian dinosaurs," which means "dinosaurs that aren't birds."

Which dinosaurs survived?
The "avian dinosaurs" (birds) were the only ones to survive the catastrophe that killed the others. They have been very successful, surviving until now and living all over the world.

But he's so ugly!

T. rex

Anchiornis

How do birds resemble dinosaurs?
Birds have evolved from reptiles. If you look at their scaly legs and beady eyes, you can see a little reptile in them! They are closest to the theropod dinosaurs—those the same shape as T. rex and Velociraptor.

CAN WE MAKE A DINOSAUR FROM A BIRD?

A dinosaur scientist in the United States is trying to make a modern dinosaur by reverse engineering—changing pieces of the DNA of birds to add dinosaur features, such as teeth in their beaks, hands instead of wings, and a tailbone.

How will this creature differ from dinosaurs?
If it works, the animal will be adapted to modern temperatures, oxygen levels, and available foods, because it will have been developed from a modern bird.

Will this bring back an extinct dinosaur?
No, because the end result won't be one of the dinosaurs that roamed the world millions of years ago, but a totally new dinosaur. It will be a slow process, changing one step at a time.

And you're sure this isn't a bit weird!?

WHAT WERE THE FIRST FOSSILS TO BE FOUND?

Where were the first US dinosaur fossils found?
The first American dinosaur fossils were found in 1854 near the Missouri River.

What about the first dino footprints?
The first dinosaur footprints were found in 1835 in Connecticut, USA. They were mistaken for giant bird footprints, because people thought all dinosaurs walked on four legs.

William Smith found a shin bone from an Iguanodon in England in 1809, but he didn't know what it was.

The first nearly complete dinosaur fossil found was a Hadrosaurus unearthed in New Jersey, USA, in 1858.

English scientist William Buckland described the first dinosaur in 1824: Megalosaurus.

In 1877, the first Brontosaurus and Stegosaurus were unearthed, both in the USA.

Who's the most scary?

Where was the first T. rex fossil found?
The first T. rex was found in 1900 in Montana, USA.

When was Tricertops discovered?
The first Triceratops fossil was discovered in 1888.

What about Diplodocus?
Diplodocus was discovered in 1899.

Still me!

HOW ARE FOSSILS FORMED?

Are complete dinosaur fossils common?
It's rare to find a whole dinosaur; most fossil finds are a few bones.

A dead animal is covered by water, and sand or mud (sediment) settles over it, preventing it from breaking up and drifting away.

More sediment piling up above squashes the material around the bones until it hardens into rock.

Why do we only find skeletons?
Usually, the soft parts rot away, leaving just the hard parts—bones, teeth, claws, and any spikes or bony plates.

Did all dinosaurs become fossils?
Very, very few dead animals turn into fossils. Most are eaten or rot away, their bones scattered and crushed.

Just occasionally, soft parts like skin or feathers fossilize.

1 What are the best conditions for forming a fossil?
If a dead dino ended up in water and was buried quickly by sediment, it just might turn into a fossil.

2 How do fossils get buried?
More and more layers of rock piled up over the years, burying the fossil deep underground.

3 What makes fossils rocky?
Over years and years, chemicals in the bones were swapped for minerals in water, and the bones became hard, like stone.

Or the bones might rot away, leaving a space that fills with minerals and makes a cast of the bones.

4 The layers of rock twist and move over time, sometimes bringing fossils to the top.

How are fossils found?
Scouring wind, rain, or tides can expose fossils near the surface.

Megalosaurus

I am pretty mega!

WHEN WERE DINOSAURS NAMED?

The word "dinosaur" was first used by the English scientist Richard Owen in 1842.

Iguanodon

Hylaeosaurus

What were the first dinosaurs to be named?
The first dinosaurs to be named—before anyone knew they were dinosaurs—were Megalosaurus in 1824 and Iguanodon in 1825. Hylaeosaurus was next, named in 1833.

Terrible lizard!? I don't think so!

What was Owen's brain wave?
Owen was the first person to spot a similarity between all three. He declared that they were part of a group of similar animals, of a type no longer found on Earth. They were something like living reptiles, though much larger. His name for them, "dinosaur," means "terrible lizard."

HOW WAS OWEN'S THEORY RECEIVED?

Only 45 years after Owen named the dinosaurs, it looked as though he might have been wrong.

Ornithischian—lizard-hipped

What had changed in the last 45 years?
Many more dinosaurs had been found and they fell into two different groups with different types of hips. One group had hips like modern birds, and the other had hips like modern lizards.

Why did scientists question the existence of dinosaurs?
The British paleontologist Harry Seeley thought the two groups were so different that they should not be grouped together at all, and that "dinosaurs" as a single group didn't exist.

It took nearly 100 years—until the 1970s—for scientists to accept that both groups came from a single ancestor and dinosaurs did exist, after all.

Saurischian—bird-hipped

WHAT WAS THE FIRST DINOSAUR FOSSIL TO BE FOUND?

The first-known dinosaur fossil was described in 1677 by Robert Plot, who ran the Ashmolean Museum in Oxford, England.

What was the fossil part of?
It was the end of a huge thigh bone. Plot guessed it belonged to a giant human at least 297 cm (9 ft 9 in) tall. He wondered if it could have come from an elephant, but decided it was the wrong shape.

What happened to the fossil?
The fossilized leg bone was lost long ago, but it's now thought to have been from a Megalosaurus.

ARE DRAGONS DINOSAURS?

Some people have wondered whether stories about dragons have come either from actual dinosaurs or from finding fossilized dinosaur bones.

Did humans live with dinosaurs?
No. Dinosaurs and humans have never overlapped, so even the earliest people could never have seen dinosaurs. There's a gap of 65 million years between the last non-bird dinosaurs and humans!

But early people could have possibly come across fossilized dinosaurs and made up dragons to explain them.

Who invented dragons?
Legends of dragons cropped up in China and Europe independently—perhaps people found dinosaur fossils in both places and came up with slightly different versions of dragons.

Weird!

Dragon?

WHAT WAS THE FIRST DINOSAUR?

It might have been Herrerasaurus, which—if it was a dinosaur—was certainly an early one. It lived 231 million years ago in South America.

What did Herrerasaurus look like?

It was around 6 m (20 ft) long but only 90 cm (3 ft) tall, with a long tail.

Herrerasaurus ran on two legs and ate meat, like the later theropods, and probably weighed about as much as a large crocodile does now.

Herrerasaurus

How did Herrerasaurus get its name?

The first fossil of Herrerasaurus was discovered accidentally by an Argentinian man looking after his goats. His name was Victorino Herrera, and the "maybe dinosaur" was named after him.

They should have called it "Goatasaurus!"

CAN DINOSAURS CLIMB?

There are dinosaur tracks going up a cliff face in Bolivia, but this doesn't mean that dinosaurs could run up a cliff face like Spider-Man.

The collection of 5,000 footprints marching 100 m (330 ft) up a limestone cliff in a quarry at Cal Orcko represents at least eight different species of dinosaur.

The tracks were made in flat ground, in the mud beside a lake where dinosaurs came to drink 68 million years ago.

The tracks were covered with mud and hardened to fossils millions of years ago.

Why do the tracks go upward?

They now go up a cliff face because the land has shifted and twisted, and the part that was horizontal is now almost vertical.

HOW DID REPTILES EVOLVE?

Reptiles evolved from amphibians—animals like frogs and toads that lay soft eggs.

Koolasuchus (amphibian)

Dimetrodon (reptile)

What's the problem with amphibian eggs?

Amphibians breathe air but lay soft, squashy eggs. The eggs would dry out on land, so amphibians have to lay their eggs in water. This means that amphibians can't stray far from rivers or the coast.

Reptiles had a new trick—they laid eggs with a thick, leathery shell that didn't dry out. It meant that reptiles could live anywhere. Reptiles soon took over from amphibians.

The archosaurs ("ruling reptiles") gave rise to dinosaurs. Birds, crocodiles, snakes, and lizards are all modern archosaurs.

Why are small dinosaur fossils rare?

Things don't fossilize easily, and most things that die never become fossils.

Small, fragile bones and skeletons are very easily broken—or even gulped down by carrion-eaters feeding on dead animals.

Few small dinosaurs get fossilized in the first place.

Big dinosaurs are pretty hard to miss, but little fossils stay hidden. The tiny Hesperonychus was first described in 2009. It was feathery and weighed about 1.9 kg (4 lb)—tiny for a dino!

WERE ALL DINOSAURS GIANTS?

There aren't many fossils of small dinosaurs, but that doesn't mean that small dinosaurs weren't around.

North America, 75 million years ago

Hesperonychus

Ha ha! I eat the little ones!

WHY DID THE DINOSAURS DIE OUT?

About 66 million years ago, the dinosaurs' world came to an end. A mass extinction event wiped out the non-bird dinosaurs and many other animals.

What caused the extinction?
The most likely culprit was an asteroid—a huge rock from space—crashing into Earth.

How big was the asteroid?
The rock was probably 10–15 km (6–9 miles) across.

It was the end of an era. Sigh.

Where did the asteroid land?
It hit Earth at the site of a crater in Chicxulub, off the coast of Mexico, discovered in 1991.

How big a crater did it make?
The crater is 180 km (112 miles) across.

Borealopelta

How many plants and animals died out?
About 75 percent of the different types of plants and animals on Earth became extinct (died out).

The impact threw dust and debris into the air that would have darkened the sky.

Did the dinosaurs die out suddenly?
Most of the animals near the impact site died within minutes or hours of the hit.

What about elsewhere?
The asteroid probably caused massive climate change that killed more plants and animals.

The crash also made a tsunami (giant wave) 100 m (328 ft) tall.

DID DINOSAURS FLY?

Although birds are modern dinosaurs, the flying animals of the dinosaur world—pterosaurs—were not dinosaurs, but flying reptiles.

What was the first pterosaur?
The earliest pterosaur was Eudimorphodon. It lived 220 million years ago in the area that's now Italy.

Did birds evolve from pterosaurs?
No—they evolved from small dinosaurs. Pterosaurs died out leaving no living relatives. They were here once, but now they're gone.

What is special about pterosaurs?
Pterosaurs were the first vertebrates (animals with backbones) that could fly. They spread to all continents and survived about 150 million years—a serious success story!

Eudimorphodon

WERE THERE ANY AQUATIC DINOS?

Although some dinosaurs could swim, most were dedicated land-lubbers. But the seas weren't empty.

Plesiosaurs and pliosaurs were more obviously reptiles, but with paddle-shaped limbs.

There were marine reptiles—reptiles that had left the land to live in the sea and had adapted to life in the water. They came in four main types.

Mosasaurs looked like crocodiles with paddles.

Ichthyosaurs were fish-shaped.

There was also a good collection of fish, sponges, arthropods (things with a hard, jointed outside like crabs and shrimp), and cephalopods (squashy things like squid).

And sea turtles were, well, turtles—much like modern sea turtles.

HOW DO PTEROSAURS COMPARE TO BIRDS?

Pterosaurs had claws part of the way along their wings.

Pterosaur wings might have attached to the hind legs.

How are pterosaurs like cats?
Some pterosaurs might have had retractable claws, as cats do.

Did pterosaurs have teeth?
Some pterosaurs had teeth in their beaks.

Most pterosaurs were much bigger than most birds.

Long-tailed pterosaurs had a bone in their tail; birds' tails are all feather.

Many pterosaurs had a spectacular head crest made of skin and bone. Birds' crests are only feathers.

Did pterosaurs build nests in trees?
Pterosaurs could not stand on branches or nest in trees.

What were pterosaur eggs like?
Pterosaur eggs probably had soft, leathery shells like turtle eggs, rather than hard shells like bird eggs.

Could pterosaurs walk?
Pterosaurs walked on all fours on the ground.

HOW BIG DID PTEROSAURS GROW?

Quetzalcoatlus was a pterosaur as tall as a giraffe. It stalked North America and soared through the skies 77-66 million years ago.

Quetzalcoatlus probably ate carrion (dead animals) and snapped up any animals it could get its long, toothless beak around, including small dinosaurs.

How heavy was Quetzalcoatlus?
Quetzalcoatlus weighed 250 kg (550 lb). This is the heaviest an animal can be and still fly, so its record won't be beaten.

How wide were its wings?
It had a small body and was mostly wings—the wingspan was nearly 12 m (40 ft), which is the size of a small plane.

DID PTEROSAURS REALLY HAVE HANDS?

Yes—their wings were hands built around a long finger.

Pteroid

The pterosaur's elbow was close to its body, the joint at the middle of the wing is the wrist, and all the longer end of the wing is an extended fourth finger.

Think I'll keep my finger as it is, thanks!

They had an extra bone pointing the other way, called the pteroid, which supported the other side of the wing. No other animal has this bone.

Skin stretched between the end of the finger and either the body or the leg. Imagine if just one of your fingers was really, really long!

Tupandactylus

Tupandactylus, a pterosaur that lived in Brazil 112 million years ago, had a ridiculously large head crest, about as big as its body.

HOW MUCH DID PTEROSAURS VARY?

Lots! In many different ways.

The largest pterosaurs often had a wingspan of more than 9 m (30 ft).

Nemicolopterus

Pteranodon

Pteranodon must have been common 85 million years ago—thousands of fossils have been found throughout North America.

Nyctosaurus had a forked crest about two-and-a-half times as long as its skull.

Nemicolopterus was one of the smallest pterosaurs. With just a 25 cm (10 in) wingspan, it was about the size of a sparrow.

Hatzegopteryx was the top predator on the island of Hațeg, now part of Romania. It even ate small sauropods.

Anhanguera

Pterosaurs like Anhanguera had frightening teeth that stuck out at odd angles— perfect for catching fish and not letting them slither away.

Caelestiventus

Hatzegopteryx

One of the largest Triassic pterosaurs was Caelestiventus, with a wingspan of 1.5 m (4.9 ft) and 110 teeth, four of them 2.5-cm (1-in) long fangs. It lived in Utah 200 million years ago.

Are birds or dinosaurs bigger?
The biggest bird today is the wandering albatross, with a wingspan of 3.5 m (11.5 ft). Pterosaurs could have been three times as big!

Wandering albatross

DID ALL PTEROSAURS HAVE TAILS?

The early pterosaurs, like Dimorphodon, had a long, bony tail that helped them to balance. Later pterosaurs, like Pterodactylus, had no tail at all or only a tiny stump of tail.

Dimorphodon

Could Dimorphodon move its tail?
The tail of pterosaurs like Dimorphodon could move from side to side, but probably didn't move up and down. Instead, it stuck out straight behind the animal.

Why was the tail useful?
It could have been used like a rudder, helping the pterosaur to turn, but it wouldn't spoil its streamlined shape by drooping and dragging.

WHAT WAS THE FIRST PTEROSAUR FOSSIL MISTAKEN FOR?

A French scientist, Georges Cuvier, decided in 1801 that pterosaurs flew through the air rather than the water.

When Italian scientist Cosimo Collini found the first pterosaur fossil in 1784, he thought he'd discovered a sea animal that used its arms as paddles.

Did pterosaurs swim?
Many of them probably did dive into the water to snatch fish or other food, but they probably didn't swim far underwater.

How did the pterodactyl get its name?
Cuvier also invented the name "ptero-dactyle," which means "winged finger." Now scientists call them pterosaurs, and Pterodactylus is just one type. Different pterosaurs lived all over the world.

AT WERE PTE OSAURS' CRESTS LIKE?

Thalassodromeus had one of the largest head crests of all, on a skull 1.4 m (4 ft 8 in) long. It lived in Brazil 100 million years ago.

Some pterosaurs had dramatic crests made of bone or another tough material, such as cartilage, covered with skin.

Thalassodromeus

I'm a crested wonder!

Were the crests patterned?
We don't know what patterns the crests showed—they might have been bright reds, blues, and yellows to attract a mate.

Were the crests solid?
Scientists aren't even sure whether some of the crests were a bony framework or filled in with a large sail-like flap of skin.

WERE THERE FLIERS BEFORE PTEROSAURS?

The pterosaurs perfected gliding and flying with wings made of skin, but they weren't the first to try it.

Coelurosauravus

Wheeee— I can fly!

Did the Coelurosauravus fly?
The lizard-like Coelurosauravus had flaps of skin sticking out from its sides that it probably used to glide between trees. It didn't quite fly—it was more like jumping with style—and its wings were stiffened with rods of bone.

Coelurosauravus was 46 cm (18 in) long and lived in Madagascar and Europe 260–251 million years ago.

The wings weren't extensions of its ribs, but special structures that have never been found in any other animal.

WHAT DID PTEROSAURS EAT?

Many types of pterosaurs lived near the coast and hunted for fish. They would soar over the sea or a river, then dive to snatch fish from near the surface.

Why was fishing risky for pterosaurs?

They weren't very good at taking off from the surface of the water after diving, and they probably had to flap and struggle for a few seconds. This gave sea predators a chance to catch them.

How did pterosaurs catch fish?

Some pterosaurs had sharp, snaggly teeth that would hold a slippery fish firmly. Others had no teeth and gulped fish straight down, like modern seabirds.

WHAT ATE PTEROSAURS?

Fossils of bone-plated fish biting down on pterosaurs show that the fish caught their prey by grabbing a wing as the pterosaur dived or tried to leave the surface of the sea.

The fact that the fish were fossilized in the act shows it didn't end well for either creature. It's likely that the fish's closely packed teeth got stuck in the leathery wing of the pterosaur, and it couldn't free itself.

Both eventually sank to the seabed where they were covered with sediment and fossilized, stuck in their struggle forever.

Sounds fishy!

WHO WAS THE BOSS OF THE CRETACEOUS SEA?

Mosasaurs were giant marine reptiles up to 15 m (50 ft) long.

Mosasaurs were the last thing you would want to meet in the sea 85–65 million years ago. With jaws 90 cm (3 ft) long and dagger-like teeth, each 7.5 cm (3 in) long, they were killing machines, the fiercest predators the seas have ever held.

How did mosasaurs swim?
Mosasaurs moved their powerful tails from side to side to drive them forward, just like sharks do. Their four paddle-like limbs helped them to steer.

How did mosasaurs hunt?
They possibly lurked among seaweed and rocks until a potential snack swam by, then lunged.

HOW FIERCE WERE MOSASAURS?

A fossil found in the African country of Angola captures a snapshot of the ferocious times of the mosasaurs.

The fossil of a large mosasaur has the bones of two smaller mosasaurs inside it—they'd been its dinner.

This is one tough cookie!

Did sharks attack mosasaurs?
There are shark teeth embedded in the fossil. A shark couldn't have tackled a mosasaur and lived, but it would scavenge a dead one. Even dead, the mosasaur was tough enough for its flesh to pull out the shark's teeth.

WHAT CAME FIRST—WATER REPTILES OR LAND REPTILES?

Water reptiles evolved from land reptiles that had evolved from amphibians that originally came out of the water. So they had gone full circle.

Animals evolve to go in and out of the water all the time. Millions of years later, mammals would make the same journey back to the sea.

Plesiosaur

Emperor penguin

Blue whale

How did whales evolve?
Today's whales and dolphins have evolved from an ancient land-lubbing mammal that was a little bit like a modern dog. And penguins are birds that have moved from land to sea.

How do sea creatures adapt?
Animals that take to the sea become more streamlined, and their limbs develop into fins or paddles.

WHO WAS FIRST TO RETURN TO WATER?

Nothosaurs were probably the first reptiles to give up life on land to head to the sea.

Nothosaur

Did nothosaurs ever go on land?
They still breathed air and probably laid eggs on land. As their feet had become paddle-shaped and probably webbed, and their legs shortened, going on land must have been a struggle for them.

How did nothosaurs swim?
It's likely that they swam using their tail in a wavy motion like a modern crocodile.

How did nothosaurs hunt?
Fossilized "foraging tracks" suggest that nothosaurs stirred mud up from the seabed with their paddle-like feet, then ate the animals they disturbed.

IS A PLACODONT MORE LIKE A TURTLE OR A WALRUS?

Early placodonts, like Placodus, were closer to the walrus-end of the spectrum.

Or they looked like it. They were one of the odder groups of marine reptiles.

Later types, like Henodus, had protective bony plates all over, making them look like rather squashed turtles.

Placodus

Why did placodonts live in water?
Being heavy would have made it hard work on land. They would have moved slowly, and those without a shell would have been at risk from predators.

What did placodonts eat?
Most ate shellfish, and most had teeth suited to pulling them from rocks and crushing their shells.

Did Henodus have teeth?
Henodus had only two teeth. It was probably a filter feeder or scraped plants off the seabed.

Henodus's shell went way beyond its limbs, making it something a little bit like a Frisbee.

How big were placodonts?
The largest placodont was just under 3 m (10 ft) long—quite small compared with other marine reptiles.

Henodus

Henodus lived near the seabed. The weight of its dense, thick bones and the bony plates meant that it was easy for it to sink to the bottom.

Did placodonts go on land too?
They laid eggs on land. The babies, like modern sea turtles, probably had to scuttle to the sea to avoid becoming a snack.

DID DINOSAURS HAVE FEATHERS?

Many theropods had feathers, and there is more and more evidence of other dinosaurs having them, too.

Were they covered with feathers?
Some dinos had just had a few quills or a plume of filaments somewhere on their bodies, while others had feathers pretty much everywhere.

Some early feathers, or proto-feathers, were something like the quills of a porcupine—which are like the central rib of a bird feather without the feathery parts. Thinner ones were filaments—hair-like strands.

Deinonychus

Were the feathers used for flying?
Most didn't use their feathers to fly. The feathers probably kept them warm, and maybe gave them a camouflaged coat to help them blend in with their surroundings.

DID DINOSAURS HAVE FLEAS?

Dinosaurs were bothered by biting bugs in just the same way that modern animals and humans are.

A fossilized flea up to 165 million years old looks as if it might have sucked dinosaur blood.

Diplodocus

Yum, yum!

Shoo flea, don't bother me!

What about ticks?
A preserved part of a dinosaur tail 100 million years old even has a tiny tick on it. A tick is an eight-legged bug that feeds on the blood of larger animals.

How big were dino fleas?
Larger than modern fleas at nearly 2.5 cm (1 in) long, these scary-looking bugs had a mouth part like a saw that could cut through thick hide.

HOW WARM WERE DINOSAURS?

Using fossilized bones from two sauropod dinosaurs, a Brachiosaurus and a Camarasaurus, scientists have figured out that the dinosaurs probably had a body temperature of 36–38°C (96.8–100.4°F).

How does that compare to humans?
That's pretty much the same temperature as a human being! A healthy human generally has a temperature of 36.5–37.5°C (97.7–99.5°F).

Were dinosaurs warm-blooded?
You're warm-blooded—your body can control its own temperature. Dinosaurs might have been warm-blooded or, they could have been cold-blooded, and kept themselves at that temperature by basking in the sunshine.

I need to cool down!

Brachiosaurus

DID DINOSAURS HAVE BAD BREATH?

Carnotaurus

The teeth of a large meat-eating dinosaur like Carnotaurus or T. rex probably trapped shreds of meat, which would have attracted bacteria. As the bacteria attacked the meat, making it rot, the dinosaur would have had really stinky breath.

Why is bad breath bad news?
The smell wasn't really the point. More importantly, next time the dinosaur bit a potential meal, bacteria would transfer to the wound.

Even if the dinosaur's dinner managed to get away, the bacteria would make for a nasty festering wound, and the victim would probably fall sick. At this point, the hungry dinosaur would come back …

I can tell you're grossed out …

WHAT IS FOSSILIZED DINOSAUR POOP CALLED?

Coprolites are fossils of the food from inside a dinosaur. They can either be food fossilized inside the dino's intestine, or after it has come out the other end—dino dung.

Coprolites can show what a dinosaur actually ate, while its teeth show what it was suited to eat. They are not always the same thing.

Coprolites

What can you learn from fossilized poop?

Scientists looking at hadrosaur dung found that although the dinos were thought to be strict vegetarians, the coprolites showed that they ate crustaceans like crabs or shrimp, and rotting wood, which probably contained insects.

These could have provided calcium, which an egg-laying dinosaur would need to form eggshells.

DID DINOSAURS WALK ON TIPTOES?

Theropod dinosaurs put only their toes on the ground, with the result that the ankle looks as though it was part of the way up the leg.

We were soooo speedy!

The first toe stuck out below the ankle but was held up off the ground, before the other three toes divided (they only had four).

Their toes spread out more than ours do, looking a little bit like bird feet.

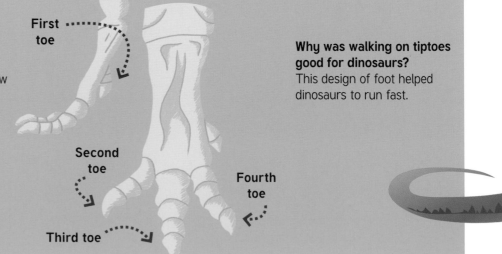

First toe

Second toe

Third toe

Fourth toe

Why was walking on tiptoes good for dinosaurs?
This design of foot helped dinosaurs to run fast.

WHICH DINOSAUR CRACKED A WHIP?

A dinosaur such as Diplodocus had a very long tail that was thin at the end.

Paleontologists believe that the animal could lash its tail so quickly that the end would be break the sound barrier, making a cracking or booming noise.

What did the dinosaur world sound like?
The prehistoric forest would have resounded to the booming, howls, growls, chattering, tweeting, and snuffling of different animals, plus the occasional crack or boom of a tail.

HOW BIG WERE SAUROPOD EGGS?

Giant sauropods could be 33 m (110 ft) long, but their eggs were just a little bigger than modern-day ostrich eggs at only 18 cm (7 in) long. This means that the hatchling dinosaurs were tiny compared to their parents—and in serious danger of being trampled or eaten by a predator.

Your egg's not dainty!

I am SO dainty!

How does that compare with an ostrich?
The largest eggs today are laid by ostriches. At more than 2 m (7 ft) tall, the ostrich is a big bird, and its eggs are 15 cm (6 in) long—but that's small relative to the size of the adult bird.

WHAT DID DINOSAURS USE THEIR CLAWS FOR?

Their claws were a different shape, and were used for grasping or pulling food toward the dinosaur's mouth or—according to some research—for digging in the ground.

Fierce theropods like Deinonychus and Baryonyx used their claws as weapons, but some plant-eating dinosaurs also had large claws.

What did they dig for?
Modern animals like anteaters and moles use their claws to dig for food, so it's fair to think that some dinos might have done the same, perhaps using them to seek out tasty roots to eat.

I wish I had a nail brush.

Nothronychus

WHAT WAS DINOSAUR VISION LIKE?

Hunters like Troodon and T. rex had eyes at the front of their head.

T. rex

The area their eyes could see had an overlap of 45–60 degrees, giving them binocular vision. That helped them to judge distance—vital if you are trying to pounce on a meal that will run away.

Do any modern-day predators have the same vision?
Birds of prey like eagles have the same arrangement of eyes at the front of a narrow head.

What about plant-eating dinos?
Plant-eating dinosaurs like Triceratops had to be on the lookout for predators, so needed a wide field of vision. They had eyes on either side of their head, so they could see almost all the way around them. They didn't need binocular vision as plants don't run away.

Triceratops

WHAT IS MYSTERIOUS ABOUT THESE THREE DINOSAURS?

Dracorex

No one has ever found any fossils of baby Pachycephalosaurus. And no one has ever found any adult fossils of Dracorex or Stygimoloch.

Stygimoloch

Pachycephalosaurus

How alike are they?
All three were thick, bone-headed animals—which is not an insult, they just had thick, bony skulls.

Who's the biggest bonehead?

When were they around?
All three lived at the same time, about 70 million years ago, in the same part of what is now North America.

What's the confusion?
Paleontologists now think they might be the same animal, but that they had different-shaped bony skulls at different stages of their life. Baby Dracorex might have grown into teenaged Stygimoloch, and finally into the boneheaded Pachycephalosaurus.

HOW DO DINO BIRDS DIFFER FROM MODERN ONES?

Dino birds might have hatched ready to fly.

What about modern birds?
Modern birds hatch either with no feathers at all, or covered with downy fluff.

Do birds need feathers to fly?
Yes, chicks that are bald stay in the nest where their parents feed them while they grow feathers.

Those with fluff can run around and feed but have to wait for their real feathers to grow in before they can fly.

How do we know that dino birds could fly from the start?
An early dinosaur-like bird found in China, called Enantiornithes, seems to have been ready to fly almost as soon as it came out of the egg.

A chick preserved in amber has flight and tail feathers already, even though it's only a few days old.

Are you sure we're ready?

DID SAUROPODS SINK OR SWIM?

If you could drop a live sauropod into water, it would bob around like a cork—sauropods were very buoyant.

Why would they float?
The air sacs in their bodies and bones made them much less dense than most animals.

I'll just paddle, thanks!

Did sauropods spend much time in water?
No. Long ago, people thought that sauropods probably spent a lot of time in water to support their weight. In fact, they would have been quite unstable in water and probably avoided deep water.

Could they swim?
They might have been all right wading, but if they swam they could easily tip over.

HOW MANY WINGS DID A MICRORAPTOR HAVE?

Some small dinosaurs like Microraptor, which lived in China 120 million years ago, had four feathery wings (and a feathered tail).

Microraptor

Where did it fit four wings?
Microraptor had long flight feathers on both the top and bottom portions of its arms and legs, giving it four true wings.

Is it a bird? Is it a plane? Nope, planes haven't been invented yet!

Could it take off?
The feathers were attached deeply, making them strong enough for flying. Microraptor could probably glide and manage powered flight, flapping its wings. It could probably even take off from the ground like a modern bird.

WHAT DID SAUROPODS LOOK LIKE?

Sauropods used to be drawn with their heads held high, often munching leaves from the tops of trees.

Now scientists think that most usually held their necks out straight in front of them like a beam—and their tails out pretty straight behind them.

Mamenchisaurus

Were all their necks straight?
No, others held neck and tail at a slant, but still pretty much in a straight line. A few, including Brachiosaurus, held their heads up most of the time.

How did they move their heads?
They could move their heads from side to side, and probably down toward the ground, but they didn't walk around with their necks held up straight.

WHAT WERE DINOSAUR FRILLS FOR?

Triceratops was just one of several dinosaurs with a head frill.

Other ceratopsians had fancy frills, too—some a lot fancier than that of Triceratops. But scientists don't agree about what they were for.

I love being all frilly!

Protoceratops

Do scientists have ideas?
The frill might have helped the dino keep cool. Warm blood might run through blood vessels in the frill where it could be cooled by the wind.

Could it have been used for showing off?
Possibly. A frill made the dino attractive to a mate, or look big and scary to a rival or a predator. The frill had bone under the skin, so it was fairly solid.

Triceratops

HOW ARE DINOSAURS LIKE BIRDS?

Microraptor

Like birds, many theropods had feathers, quills, or fluff.

Unlike birds, theropods had teeth and a bone in their tail.

How did dino birds take off?
The earliest dino birds probably ran along the ground and launched themselves for short glides or flights.

Microraptor

The dinosaurs that lived more than 65 million years ago are called non-avian (or "non-bird") dinosaurs.

Small theropod dinosaurs like Microraptor and Anchiornis looked very much like modern birds.

Anchiornis

Ichthyornis

Like birds, theropods walked on two legs.

What type of dinosaurs are modern-day birds?
Modern birds are theropod dinosaurs—the same type of dinosaur as T. rex and Velociraptor.

When did birds first appear?
The point at which some dinosaurs can start to be called birds is around 150 million years ago.

Ostrich

Velociraptor

Which modern-day birds look like dinosaurs?
Some modern birds look very much like traditional theropods. An ostrich is very dinosaur-like!

HOW MANY TOES DID DINOSAURS HAVE?

Most people have five toes on each foot and five fingers on each hand, but dinos were different.

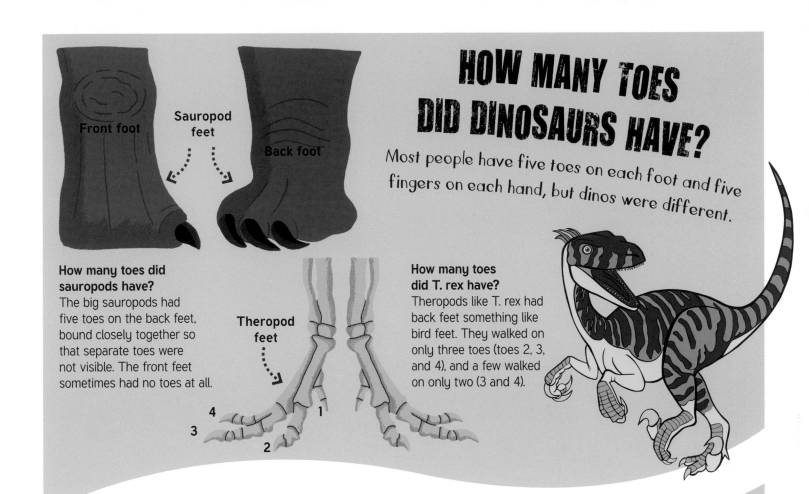

Front foot

Sauropod feet

Back foot

Theropod feet

4

3

2

1

How many toes did sauropods have?

The big sauropods had five toes on the back feet, bound closely together so that separate toes were not visible. The front feet sometimes had no toes at all.

How many toes did T. rex have?

Theropods like T. rex had back feet something like bird feet. They walked on only three toes (toes 2, 3, and 4), and a few walked on only two (3 and 4).

WHAT DID MUSEUMS GET WRONG ABOUT DINOSAURS?

Next time you see a mounted Ankylosaurus or Stegosaurus fossil in a museum, take a look at the feet.

Stegosaurus

Ankylosaurus

Most museums position them with their toes spread out on the ground. But that's not how they were in life.

What were ankylosaur and stegosaur feet like?

They had feet like those of sauropods, with their bones arranged in a semicircle that took the weight of the dino as it moved.

Could they use their toes?

The very short toes weren't used to push off from the ground. At least some of the toes were tipped with a hard hoof, and the animals effectively walked on their tiptoes—like ballerinas dancing on pointes!

WHAT CAN SCIENTISTS LEARN FROM DINO BONES?

Lots. For example, short thigh bones and long lower legs mean fast-running dinosaurs.

Can bones tell you a dino's age?
A band of different bone around the outside of the bones can show that a dinosaur had stopped growing (was an adult). That's pretty handy for dinosaur scientists!

Can you spot injuries from bones?
We can see all kinds of injuries in dinosaur bones—even possible evidence of arthritis.

Looks like this one had a toothache!

Were dinosaurs brainy?
Not really. Though some had pretty small brains, others were brainier.

Plateosaurus could clench its fists.

Plateosaurus

Dinosaurs didn't have kneecaps.

Sauropods' ankles were short—they couldn't flex their feet up and down.

How long did it take for sauropods to reach their full size?
Even the biggest sauropods reached full size by the age of 40.

HOW MANY BABIES DID DINOSAUR PARENTS HAVE?

A fossilized nest of Psittacosaurus in China has 34 baby skeletons beneath a parent.

Sitting on all these eggs hurts my bottom!

Psittacosaurus

How do we know Psittacosaurus parents looked after their babies?
The babies had bony bones. Bones are pretty flexible in most baby animals, being largely cartilage, but become harder and bonier (ossified) as the babies grow. Their bony bones show that Psittacosaurus parents stayed with their young.

Is 34 a lot of babies for one dinosaur?
It is for one couple. It's possible that they had a communal child care system. Modern ostriches do the same, with the whole flock looking after all the chicks.

What do the baby Psittacosaurus teeth tell us about their diet?
The fossilized baby skeletons had worn teeth, suggesting that they fed themselves from an early age.

WERE DINOSAURS IN TROUBLE BEFORE THE ASTEROID HIT?

We know that all the non-bird dinosaurs died off after a catastrophic event 66 million years ago. But some of them were already in trouble.

Don't look at me

Where's everyone gone?

In North America, the number of types of ceratopsians and hadrosaurs had plunged in the previous few million years, and there was only one type of large theropod left—T. rex. Elsewhere, though, dinosaur diversity held up well.

What were their troubles before the asteroid strike?
Possibly, local conditions in North America gave dinos there a bad time. Sea levels were falling, and good, rich habitats around the coast became inland areas. It also became colder. No more sunny trips to the beach for the dinos …

How can scientists know who owned the nests?

Experts can tell from the embryos' tiny teeth that they were titanosaurs.

What are the eggs like?

Some eggs are so well preserved that even the skin of the dinosaur embryos is intact.

WHERE IS THE LARGEST DINOSAUR NEST SITE?

Nests belonging to giant titanosaurs have been discovered at Auca Mahuida, Argentina.

Was it a busy nest site?

Yes. Thousands of sauropod mothers laid their eggs in the same place.

How big were the titanosaurs?

The adult dinosaurs were up to 14 m (45 ft) long.

How many eggs are in each nest?

Some nests contain 30–40 eggs—that's a lot of small dinos to keep an eye on!

Are the nests close together?

Yes, they're just 2–3 m (6.5–10 ft) apart.

How did the nests become fossilized?

The site was in a river plain, and the nests and eggs were buried in mud when the river flooded.

How big were the newborn dinos?

The huge mothers had babies smaller than a human baby at just 38 cm (15 in) long.

How many dino eggs are at the site?

There are thousands of eggs fossilized at Auca Mahuida.

How did dino babies break out of their eggs?

The embryos have an egg tooth—a tiny spike on the end of their snout to help them break out of the egg, just as birds do now.

Were dino eggs incubated?

Nests with pieces of fossilized plants suggest that heat from rotting vegetation kept the eggs warm.

WERE SAUROPODS STRICT VEGGIES?

We always think of sauropods as being strictly vegetarian, but they hadn't all read the rules.

I'm sure I saw a snack here somewhere!

Plateosaurus

What were their teeth like?
Plateosaurus and Massospondylus had a mix of leaf-shaped teeth suited to shredding plants and pointed, cone-shaped teeth better for eating meat.

So did they eat other animals?
Some of the early sauropodomorphs, like Plateosaurus and Massospondylus, might well have snacked on small animals occasionally if they had the chance.

They also had inward-facing hands with claws that would have helped them to grab small animals.

Did dino meat-eaters also eat plants?
Similarly, some theropods might have eaten plants at times. Animals that can eat plants or other animals are called "omnivores."

Gulp!

Adult Massospondylus walked upright on two legs, which means the babies were walking on all fours until they got their balance on two legs—just as human babies do.

DID DINO BABIES CRAWL?

Handprints made by a baby Massospondylus show that the babies walked on all fours.

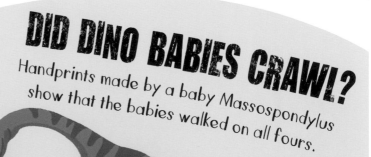

Massospondylus

How small were the babies?
Although a parent Massospondylus grew to 6 m (20 ft), the babies were tiny. They came from eggs just 6–7 cm (2.3–2.7 in) wide.

When were these dinos around?
Massospondylus lived around 200 million years ago in Africa. They are some of the oldest dinosaur embryos ever found.

WHAT WAS ODD ABOUT DINOSAUR EYES?

Many dinosaurs had bony rings in their eyes called scleral rings, which supported the iris of the eye.

Can we tell how big dinosaur eyes were?

Obviously, dinosaurs couldn't have bone blocking the pupil (where light enters the eye), or they couldn't see. The gap in the middle of the ring gives us some idea of the size of the dino's eye.

scleral rings

What does a large ring mean?

In 2011, some scientists suggested that a larger ring might mean that the dinosaur was active at night. Those they identified as nighttime dinosaurs turned out to be hunters, and daytime dinosaurs with smaller rings included the plant-eating sauropods.

So, dinosaurs were night hunters?

Not all dinosaur scientists accept the conclusion, but today many predators hunt at night or dusk, so it seems possible.

DID MICRORAPTOR HAVE NIGHT VISION?

Microraptor seems to have had large eyes—at least, it had a large space in the scleral bone for light to get into its eyes.

Why was nighttime good for a Microraptor?

It would make sense for Microraptor to hunt at night because it was quite small and ate other small sleeping animals that it could snap up easily. And it wouldn't want to be stepped on by stomping great dinosaurs out in the daytime.

What makes it seem less likely?

On the other hand, Microraptor apparently had iridescent feathers. Birds with iridescent feathers are rarely nocturnal. There's not much point having shimmery feathers if you only come out in the dark. So when did Microraptor go out? No one is really sure.

Hey! Careful!

Microraptor

WHAT CAN YOU KNOW FROM A DINOSAUR NOSE?

We can learn about how it ate. Some meat-eaters like Velociraptor had a long, narrow snout with jaws that moved up and down like scissors.

Velociraptor

You won't like me when I'm hungry!

Baryonyx

What did a long snout offer?
These could make quick, slashing bites to weaken an animal that the dino wanted to eat. Some with a very narrow snout, like Baryonyx, snapped fish out of the water like a crocodile does.

What about wide jaws?
Those with a massive, wide jaw could crunch down with force. T. rex had a mouth strong enough to bite through bone. It could rip open carcasses and even eat the bones. Shards of bone fragments found in their fossilized dung show that they did!

WHAT ARE SQUARE JAWS FOR?

Today, animals such as rhinos with a wide, square jaw are often grazers—they eat grass and other ground-level plants.

Diplodocus

Was it the same for dinosaurs?
It's easy to see that short, stocky dinosaurs like Ankylosaurus probably ate ground-growing plants— they couldn't reach the treetops!

What about giants like Diplodocus?
Diplodocus also had a wide mouth. This suggests it didn't always need its long neck to reach high into the trees, but might have eaten low-growing plants, too.

Are there any other clues to a Diplodocus diet?
Tiny pits worn into Diplodocus's teeth are further evidence for ground-level eating. Such tooth damage often comes from accidentally picking up grit along with plants from the ground.

43

WHAT CAN WE LEARN FROM A DINO'S FULL BELLY?

We can learn about what they ate.

Archosaurs are yummy!

Coelophysis

Most meals inside are found in theropods. Coelophysis was found with small archosaurs inside.

A lizard was found inside a German Compsognathus, and a Sinosauropteryx in China had died after eating a small mammal.

What did Microraptor eat?
One Microraptor was found to have eaten a fish. This meant that paleontologists had to rethink their idea that Microraptor spent most of its time in trees. As well as gliding and climbing, it was clearly spending at least some of its time near the water.

What did a Baryonyx have in its belly?
A Baryonyx has been found with a belly full of fish scales as well as a young Iguanodon-type dinosaur.

WHICH DINOSAUR HID IN A MUSEUM FOR 50 YEARS?

The fossil of Nyasasaurus, possibly the oldest dinosaur, was found in the 1930s but only correctly described in 2013.

Nyasasaurus

The first person to write about Nyasasaurus, in 1956 thought it was an archosaur. So, although scientists had the fossil and knew it existed, they didn't know it was a dinosaur—if it was!

If Nyasasaurus really is a dinosaur, it is much older than the next oldest, pushing back the date of dinosaur evolution by 12 million years. But dinosaurs could be even older than that. Footprints found in Poland were made by dinosaur-shaped animals 249 million years ago.

44

WHO STOLE THE POOP?

Dung beetles! They collect, feed on, and break down the dung produced by other animals. Without them, the world would be completely covered in animal droppings.

Did dung beetles get enough to eat?
In the time of the dinosaurs, dung beetles had giant feasts, as some dinosaur droppings are 60 cm (2 ft) long. Sauropods would have dropped great piles of sloppy dung, too.

Plenty to work with here!

Did dung beetles leave traces?
Some dung fossils have holes that show where dung beetles have taken some dung, or worms and other animals have burrowed through it. With food that's hard to digest, such as tough plant material, up to half of the goodness was still left in the food after it went through the dino's gut.

COULD DINOSAURS SWIM?

Dinosaurs almost all lived on land, but some could probably swim if they had to.

So, did Triceratops sink?
Clusters of Triceratops fossils found together suggest that sometimes the animals were drowned by flash floods.

Is swimming easy for large animals?
Today, elephants and wolves live on land, but they can swim and are even quite good at it. Some dinosaurs were just the wrong shape and weight, though.

Could a Triceratops swim?
Dinosaurs like Triceratops were very heavy at the front and had a short neck with a down-pointing head. It's unlikely that Triceratops could have lifted its hefty head high enough to breathe when in the water.

The water looks a little wet to me.

HOW DID DINO BIRDS LEARN TO FLY?

How did they start flying?
There are three ideas for how they evolved to fly. They might have jumped from trees and glided.

As they did more flapping, they got stronger chest muscles.

Or they might have scrambled up slopes, trees, or cliffs, flapping their wings to go faster.

How did birds evolve?
Birds evolved from maniraptors as their bodies changed to adapt to new lifestyles.

How did they take off?
They might have run along the ground, flapping their wings until they took off.

How did feathers help?
Feathers definitely helped with flying—so nearly all birds got more feathery and their feathers became fuller, as flying became more important.

Did feathers lead to birds?
Feathers didn't start because animals wanted to fly—feathers were repurposed when flying evolved.

Were long feathers best?
Those with longer wing feathers flew better, so longer feathers became more common.

46

WHO MUNCHED ON FLOWERS?

Triceratops and Stegosaurus ate flowers and other parts of flowering plants. Flowering plants appeared later in the dinosaurs' reign, so only some dinos got to feast on bouquets of flowers.

Stegosaurus

Why would flowers get eaten?

Flowering plants are low growing, so they were ideal for grazing dinosaurs. The number of ornithischian dinosaurs toward the end of the Cretaceous increased dramatically—at exactly the same time flowering plants (called "angiosperms") were spreading widely. The two seem to have gone together.

Were flowers easy to eat?

The ornithischians had good teeth for slicing and chopping, and the angiosperms were softer than the conifer needles high in the trees, so flowering plants were a good meal for ornithischians.

HOW DID SAUROPODS KEEP THEIR EGGS WARM?

At least some sauropods made use of the heat naturally produced by the Earth's underground activity to keep their eggs warm.

Were eggs heated from below?

At a nest site in Argentina, nests are found 1–3 m (3–10 ft) from active geysers—natural hot springs and water spouts with water warmed underground by scalding-hot magma. The nests had natural underfloor heating!

What did the nest site look like?

When it was in use 134–110 million years ago, the nest site would have looked like some parts of Yellowstone Park in the USA do now, with steam, fumes, and hot water coming from holes in the ground.

DID DINOSAURS LIVE IN BURROWS?

Some small ones probably did. In Australia and in Montana, USA, paleontologists have found fossilized burrows apparently dug by small plant-eating dinosaurs.

How big is a dinosaur burrow?
The Australian burrow is 2 m (7 ft) long and has a diameter of 30 cm (12 in).

Scientists tested the theory that the single adult and two young dinosaurs found fossilized in a den had died in a burrow that then filled with sediment and preserved their bodies. They made an identical burrow system with PVC pipes and used rabbit skeletons in place of dinosaurs.

Which dinosaurs lived underground?
The only identified burrowing dinosaur is *Oryctodromeus cubicularis* from North America.

Oryctodromeus cubicularis

HOW LONG DID DINO EGGS TAKE TO HATCH?

Scientists used to assume that dinosaur eggs, like bird eggs, hatched fairly quickly—in maybe three weeks or so. But it seems that they took much longer—up to six months.

How did scientists figure this out?
Scientists discovered how long it took dinosaur embryos to grow by examining the tiny teeth of ornithischian dinosaurs preserved inside eggs.

Can you discover a dinosaur's age from its teeth?
Scientists found that teeth have miniature growth rings, with new layers that were laid down each day. Counting the layers shows how long the tooth had been growing.

Mei
long

HOW DID DINOSAURS GO TO SLEEP?

It's hard to know how most dinosaurs slept, so nobody knows for sure.

Zzzzzz

Why is it hard to know?
Unless we find fossils of dinos that died in their sleep, we can't tell—and sometimes we wouldn't be able to tell anyway. If a dinosaur slept standing up, we wouldn't even know it had died while sleeping.

Did dinosaurs sleep like birds?
At least some of them slept curled up on the ground or in a nest. Two fossils of *Mei long*, a tiny, feathery Chinese dinosaur with big eyes, were found with their heads resting over their folded arms and their tails wrapped around their bodies.

Birds don't have a long tail to wrap around, but they do sleep with their head over their shoulder.

DID VOLCANOES HELP WIPE OUT THE DINOSAURS?

Massive, long-term volcanic eruptions must have been hard to live through—even without a rock from space.

What did long-lasting eruptions do?
Massive volcanic eruptions that went on for hundreds of thousands of years were already changing the climate. They were creating the Deccan Traps in India— the other side of the world from the asteroid strike.

Could dinosaurs have avoided disasters?
Dinosaurs might have survived an asteroid or eruptions, but with terrible events on both sides of the world, it was too much for them. Or at least for all except the birds that could fly from place to place to find food and nest sites.

Oh, man!

Rajasaurus

DID DINOSAURS LIVE IN HERDS?

Fossil tracks show that some dinosaurs moved together in large groups. Today, some animals like to live in large groups, like flocks of sheep or herds of bison.

I want to be in the middle.

There are tracks that have the footprints of many sauropods all moving in the same direction at the same time.

Why is being in a group helpful?
Being in a big group is a good way of staying safe from predators. Modern prey animals like antelope and gazelles do this. For each individual, it cuts the chances of being eaten.

Move over!

DID RAPTORS HUNT IN PACKS?

Just as dinosaurs that are likely to be dinner huddled together to stay safe, the dinos that wanted to eat them might have hunted together.

Do we have proof of hunting packs?
Several fossil groups show a number of raptors—Deinonychus and Utahraptor, in different cases—apparently caught in the act of attacking or eating large prey together.

Deinonychus

Did large dinos hunt in packs?
Ganging up would have helped small dinosaurs tackle larger prey. It's not known whether huge animals like T. rex ever hunted in groups. That would have been a scary sight!

Where shall we hunt today?

HOW DID TREES AVOID BEING EATEN?

Animals and plants often evolve together, either helping each other or trying to win the race to eat or avoid being eaten.

Many trees in the age of the dinosaurs had long trunks and only grew branches high up. This meant that most animals couldn't reach up high enough to eat their leaves, and that was good for the trees.

Couldn't sauropods reach up high to eat them?
Sauropods grew very large, with very long necks—so they could reach. But even they could probably reach only the lower branches of most trees.

Brachiosaurus

Was there a balance?
Dinner and diner must have reached a balance where the trees could survive being nibbled at their lower end and dinosaurs could find enough to eat.

> Munch, munch!

HOW MUCH DID DINOSAURS EAT?

Big plant-eating dinosaurs needed a lot of food.

Are leaves and twigs a good dino diet?
The most plentiful plant foods are leaves, twigs, and bark, but they're not very good foods. There's not much goodness in them, and they take a lot of energy to digest.

What did plant-eaters do?
The poor quality of their food meant that dinos needed a huge amount, so they had to eat nearly all the time.

Any better snacks?
Good quality foods like fruit, seeds, and roots are easier to digest and have more concentrated nutrition, but there were fewer of them.

What could live on seeds?
Only small dinos could live on this kind of food. Most of a tree is leaves and twigs, not fruit or seeds. And digging up the roots kills a plant.

> What are you up to after breakfast?

> Um ... my second breakfast.

WHAT CAN FOSSILS TELL US ABOUT DINOSAUR LIVES?

One fossil of a pterosaur bone with a spinosaur tooth in it suggests the spinosaur probably snapped at it.

Ouch!

Is there a fossil fight?
A deadly fight is preserved in a fossil from Montana, USA— a large theropod has 26 teeth embedded in a plant-eater, but its own skull has been cracked.

How about fossilized footprints?
Footprints around fossil tree trunks in Utah show where a group of dinos dined on leaves.

Footprints record a dinosaur "stampede" in Australia, when a large group of small dinosaurs all ran away from something at the same time.

Can fossils tell us about a dinosaur's speed?
A set of dinosaur footprints in Oxford, England, shows how the length of the dino's stride changed as it walked and then ran.

A set of footprints in Arizona shows a parent theropod and a baby walking side by side.

Tracks in Texas, USA, show that at least one theropod was hunting a group of sauropods more than 100 million years ago.

What secrets does poop hide?
The size and shape of dino dung fossils tell scientists about the size and shape of the dinosaur's gut and butt.

Do fossils hide broken bones?
A Mongolian fossil shows a Velociraptor with its claw stuck in the neck of a Protoceratops about the size of a sheep. The Velociraptor's arm has been broken.

Do fossils reveal who eats whom?
Fossils of Tenontosaurus with lots of Deinonychus teeth around suggest that Tenontosaurus was a snack Deinonychus especially liked.

Tenontosaurus

I am not a snack!

WHAT DOES THE NAME T. REX MEAN?

The name *Tyrannosaurus rex* means "king tyrant lizard."

Could a T. rex sniff you out?
T. rex had an excellent sense of smell—so hiding wouldn't help something escape from it.

How long were T. rex teeth?
The largest T. rex teeth were 30 cm (1 ft) long.

Did T. rex stand upright?
People originally drew T. rex standing upright with its tail on the floor.

In fact, it held its body and tail horizontally, balancing its huge head.

Did T. rex have a big head?
The biggest T. rex skull is 1.2 m (4 ft) long.

Microscopic lines inside a T. rex tooth show how the tooth built up day by day—like tree rings.

How big is the largest T. rex discovered?
The largest T. rex found is nicknamed "Sue." She was 12.8 m (42 ft) long and 3.66 m (12 ft) tall. Discovered in 1990, she is the most complete and best-preserved T. rex fossil ever found.

How large was a T. rex eye?
Each of T. rex's eyeballs was the size of a grapefruit.

How heavy was a T. rex?
An adult T. rex could weigh 8,000 kg (17,600 lb).

Were T. rex babies big too?
A T. rex hatchling was no bigger than a pigeon.

How long were T. rex claws?
Each rear claw was about 18 cm (7 in) long.

HOW FAST WAS T. REX?

T. rex could move at about 29 km/h (18 mph).

How do scientists know this?
Paleontologists use scans of dinosaur bones to build computer models of parts of their bodies. From leg and hip bones, they can tell where muscles attached to the bones. By comparing them with modern animals they can figure out how large their muscles were and how they moved.

Is this fast for an animal?
It isn't super-speedy, but T. rex could run fast enough to catch its dinner.

I'd be so fast if I wasn't stuck to this base!

Who would win in a race—T. rex or an elephant?
Had there been elephants around, T. rex could have caught one—an elephant's top speed is just 24 km/h (15 mph).

WHICH IS BIGGEST— T. REX OR GIGANOTOSAURUS?

A T. rex weighed about 8,000 kg (18,000 lb) and a Giganotosaurus weighed 9,000 kg (20,000 lb).

What's 1,000 kg (2,000 lb) between friends? Giganotosaurus was the largest meat-eating dino in South America (but not quite in the whole world).

I'm so fierce right now!

Was Giganotosaurus faster than T. rex?
It beat T. rex in nearly all regards, Giganotosaurus evolved 30 million years earlier and could run faster than its more famous cousin.

Was Giganotosaurus better in every way?
No. Its brain was small—only half the size of T. rex's brain, relative to its body size, so it probably wasn't the brightest. With its size and ferocity, it didn't really need to be smart.

WHAT WERE T. REX TEETH LIKE?

T. rex had between 50 and 60 teeth the size of a banana. The longest teeth were around 30 cm (12 in) long.

"You're lucky I'm a fossil!"

Were its teeth sharp?
They were pointed and had serrated edges, like a saw-edged steak knife. That made them perfect for slicing through flesh.

Did T. rex have a strong bite?
Not only did it have huge saw-blade teeth, but it also had the most powerful bite of any land animal ever.

It could chomp down with a force ten times that of a modern alligator. But the prehistoric shark Megalodon was even more awesome, with a bite three times as powerful as that of T. rex.

Could it gobble up a human?
A human being would be just two mouthfuls for a T. rex. It's lucky that no people were around at the same time.

DID T. REX HAVE A SILLY WALK?

"Who thinks I've got a big behind?!"

Studies of dinosaur skeletons suggest that big dinos like T. rex couldn't run very fast, but they could probably reach a fair speed by "power walking"—taking normal walking-size steps, but quickly. (Running involves taking larger strides.)

How can you tell?
T. rex had big muscles in its buttocks and not much muscle in its ankles. Usually, animals with less muscly ankles can't run fast.

So, T. rex was a power walker?
T. rex's big behind combined with not-so-muscly ankles matches the kind of muscle distribution that human power walkers develop, suggesting that T. rex might have picked up speed by taking very fast small steps.

It probably looked a little silly, but who would be brave enough to laugh?

T. rex

WAS T. REX RECOGNIZED IMMEDIATELY?

No. The first three T. rex fossils found were originally thought to be from three different kinds of dinosaur. One was found in 1892, one in 1900, and one in 1902.

What was T. rex almost called?
The bones from 1902 and 1900 were first described in that order, calling the first *Tyrannosaurus rex* and the second *Dynamosaurus imperiosus.* The bone from 1892 wasn't recognized as the same animal, so missed out.

I am cool!

How did T. rex win?
When scientists realized they were the same animal, they followed the tradition of using the first name given to the animal, not the name of the fossil found first, so it became T. rex.

If they had been described in the order in which they were found, we would now talk about D. imperiosus, which is just not as snappy.

HOW FAST DID T. REX GROW?

Between the ages of 14 and 18, T. rex put on a huge amount of weight—around 2 kg (4.4 lb) a day, doubling its weight in four years.

How do scientists measure dino growth?
Scientists can see the patterns of growth spurts in dinosaurs by looking at their bones. These have growth rings, just as trees do.

Dinosaurs had to get from teeny, tiny eggs—no bigger than a football for even the largest dinos—to enormous adult bodies.

An adult T. rex could weigh 5,700 kg (nearly 12,500 lb), so the babies had a lot of growing to do.

I haven't grown fat, it's a growth spurt!

Why do bones get thicker?
During a growth spurt, the dinosaur put on a lot of bone thickness to support its heavier body.

WHAT WAS THE BIGGEST-EVER DINOSAUR?

It may have been Dreadnoughtus. The largest Dreadnoughtus fossil ever found was not even from a fully grown dinosaur, so no one is quite sure just how big it might have become.

How long was Dreadnoughtus' tail?
Its tail was 9 m (30 ft) long—it was long, strong, and flexible.

Dreadnoughtus

How big was Dreadnoughtus?
Even pre-adult, it's neck was 11 m (36 ft) long, which is as long as a telephone pole. And the bones in its neck were each nearly 1 m (more than 3 ft) across.

Where did Dreadnoughtus live?
Dreadnoughtus lived in Argentina 75 million years ago.

WHO WAS MORE SQUIRREL THAN DINOSAUR?

With a long tail covered in bushy filaments like fur, and a shorter coat over its whole body, Sciurumimus must have looked more like a savage squirrel than a regular dinosaur.

When did Sciurumimus live?
This little dinosaur, around 90 cm (3 ft) long, lived in Germany 150 million years ago. It was the first of a particular group of theropods to have been found with feathers.

A feathery squirrel reptile?

What does this tell us about feathered dinosaurs?
That feathers or fuzz evolved quite a long way back in the dinosaur family tree. Maybe a lot more dinosaurs were feathery or fuzzy than scientists have suspected.

Sciurumimus

WAS A DINOSAUR NAMED AFTER A MOUSE?

When dinosaur-hunter José Fernando Bonaparte found the fossils of a tiny sauropod-like dinosaur in Argentina, he named it Mussaurus after the Latin "mus" for mouse.

I wonder if the Mussaurus likes cheese?

Was it a tiny dino?
No. The fossils he had found were just babies, and a fully grown Mussaurus was much bigger and less mouse-like.

Mussaurus

How big was Mussaurus?
Although the babies were just 20 cm (8 in) long, the adults might have grown to 3 m (10 ft). That's still small for a sauropod, but it's way too big for a mouse.

When did Mussaurus live?
Mussaurus lived 228–208 million years ago and was a sauropodomorph. That means it was a sauropod-shaped animal, but it wasn't a fully qualified sauropod.

WHICH DINOSAUR WAS IGNORED FOR 50 YEARS?

Pegomastax. Its fossil was left in a cupboard for half a century.

How can you forget a dinosaur?
Many new dinosaurs are discovered out in the rocks, but some have been lurking unstudied in museums for decades.

Not very pretty though, is it?

What happened to Pegomastax?
A fossil dug up in the 1960s lay hidden in storage for 50 years before someone took a good look at it in 2012. It's now called Pegomastax.

Pegomastax

What was Pegomastax like?
Pegomastax was about the size of a cat. It had bristles, a beak like a parrot, and ran on two legs.

Have we missed more dinos?
Very likely. More than four-fifths of the dinosaurs known today have been named since 1990 and fossil-hunters keep finding more.

WHICH DINOSAUR WAS BELIEVED TO BE FAKE?

It's a wacky dinosaur fossil from Mongolia that looks like a cross between a duck, a penguin, and a Velociraptor.

Halszkaraptor

Was Halszkaraptor like?
Halszkaraptor had a duck-like beak packed with needle-sharp teeth, a long neck like a swan, feet with claws like a Velociraptor, and front limbs that could have been penguin-like flippers.

No wonder experts thought that it had been stuck together from parts of other dinosaurs!

There's nothing fake about me!

Is it possible that it was fake?
The fossil was still partly stuck in rock when experts got hold of it, so if it was a fake, someone put a lot of work into it. A scan showed that it is all the same dinosaur, though, so it is real.

WHICH DINOSAUR WAS A GOOD SIZE FOR A SNACK?

The little dinosaur Aquilops was about the size of a raven, which could have made it a handy-sized snack for large predators.

How did Aquilops avoid being eaten?
Aquilops had a head full of spikes to put predators off. A little like a modern thorny lizard, it would have been an uncomfortable mouthful.

You wouldn't want a mouthful of me!

Aquilops

Why is Aquilops important?
Aquilops was the earliest ceratopsian of its type found in North America by 20 million years. (Ceratopsians were plant-eating dinosaurs with a beak-like mouth and horns, including Triceratops.)

Aquilops is more closely related to ceratopsians from China than North America. This suggests a land route from China to North America 100 million years ago.

WHAT HAPPENED IF A DIPLODOCUS LOST A TOOTH?

Could you pet a Diplodocus?
Diplodocus would have been scratchy to pet—sauropods had rough hexagonal scales about 3 cm (1.2 in) across.

Did a Diplodocus have spines?
It had a row of conical spines along its tail and possibly its back, the largest 18 cm (7 in) tall.

Diplodocus replaced one of its teeth every 35 days. It had up to five teeth waiting behind every functioning tooth, ready to move forward when needed.

How long was a Diplodocus?
It was 24 m (79 ft) long.

How much did it weigh?
Diplodocus weighed 12,000 kg (26,000 lb).

Who is the most famous Diplodocus?
The Diplodocus that was displayed in London's Natural History Museum for many years was nicknamed "Dippy." It went on a tour around the British Isles from 2018 to 2021.

Diplodocus was discovered by 1877 and named in 1878.

Is there more than one "Dippy"?
American industrialist Andrew Carnegie had eight casts made of this Diplodocus and gave them to museums in Europe, Russia, and Argentina.

What were its feet like?
Diplodocus had a large claw on one toe of the front foot, and no claws on the others. No one knows what it used the claw for.

HOW FAR SOUTH DID DINOS LIVE?

Fossils of the small ornithischian dinosaur Leaellynasaura are found in Australia, but Australia was much farther south and connected to Antarctica when Leaellynasaura scurried along.

Leaellynasaura had to live for weeks on end in the gloomy half-light or dark of the Antarctic winter.

What big eyes you have.

Leaellynasaura

All the better to see you with!

Why didn't Leaellynasaura move to see daylight?
While larger dinosaurs could have migrated to areas with more daylight, Leaellynasaura was too small to migrate.

How did Leaellynasaura cope with the dark?
Just 1–2 m (39–78 in) long, Leaellynasaura probably had large eyes to deal with low levels of light.

Although Antarctica wasn't as cold as it is now, it still had a long, dark winter.

WHICH DINO HAD A SUPER-SPIKY NECK?

The small sauropod Amargasaurus from Argentina had a double row of nine spikes growing from its neck bones.

What did the spikes look like?
It's possible that the spikes were joined by skin to make a sail. The largest, in the middle of the neck, were 60 cm (24 in) long. That's quite big for a dino about 9 m (30 ft) long.

Amargasaurus

No one knows for sure what Amargasaurus used its spikes for.

Perhaps they made it less likely that a savage theropod would bite it on the back of the neck, or maybe they were used to scare rivals or attract a mate, especially if there was a sail—or two sails.

WHICH DINOSAUR WAS A REAL SHOW-OFF?

Epidexipteryx was a tiny dinosaur that weighed little more than an apple, but had really fancy feathers at the back end.

What was special about Epidexipteryx?
It had four long, fancy feathers that stuck up out of its rump.

When did Epidexipteryx live?
It lived about 168–152 million years ago in China, where it scampered over the ground, probably eating insects, lizards, and other small creatures.

Were its feathers used for flying?
No. They were probably used for impressing other Epidexipteryx—particularly potential girl-Epidexipteryx-friends.

Scientists think that it might have used its tail like a peacock does, to make a big, fancy "look at me" display.

Yes, I know. I am pretty spectacular!

Epidexipteryx

WERE ANKYLOSAURS BORN WITH THEIR SPIKES?

Ankylosaurs didn't hatch with all their bony plates in place; they became bonier as they grew, starting at the front.

I'm so sturdy!

In particular, they didn't have their bony tail clubs until they were grown up.

Ankylosaur

I'm on the way to getting sturdy!

Why did adults have bony tail clubs?
They may have used them in squabbles with other ankylosaurs, as well as to thwack hungry predators.

This type of squabble, for a mate, territory, or control of a group, only happens when an animal is fully grown.

HOW TOUGH WAS AN ANKYLOSAURUS?

A large Ankylosaurus could swing its bony tail club hard enough to break the leg bones of a T. rex.

How heavy was Ankylosaurus?
Ankylosaurus weighed as much as two modern rhinos.

What does the name Ankylosaurus mean?
Its name means "fused lizard."

How long was Ankylosaurus?
It grew to 6.25 m (20.5 ft) long.

Have many Ankylosauruses have been found?
Only three Ankylosaurus fossils have been found, and none is complete.

Would a predator have attacked an Ankylosaurus?
Ankylosaurus had thick bony knobs and plates embedded in the skin over most of its body and head, making it pretty much bite-proof.

A predator would have to get underneath or tip it over to bite it, because the belly had no osteoderms.

Was Ankylosaurus a fast runner?
Even in a hurry, an ankylosaur couldn't get above 9 km/h (6 mph).

What did an Ankylosaurus eat?
An Ankylosaurus had a parrot-like beak, a strong, muscular tongue, and teeny-tiny teeth. It ate low-growing plants—including flowers.

Did it use its tail club to attack?
Its fierce-looking tail club was only used to defend it against meat-eaters, not for attacks.

63

DID AN ANKYLOSAURUS CARRY A CLUB?

Yes. The bony club was around 60 cm (2 ft) across.

Could Ankylosaurus swing its club?
Yes. To help swing it, the last few vertebrae (back bones) in Ankylosaurus's tail were fused together, and it had ossified (turned-to-bone) tendons in the tail. This made a sturdy rod inside the tail that didn't bend but acted as a straight handle, ending with the club.

Was the club heavy?
Yes, and its weight probably limited the size it could grow to.

What was the club made of?
The club itself was made of fused, interlocking osteoderms (little bony lumps).

HOW DID ANKYLOSAURUS GET ITS STRANGE TAIL?

Could using its club tail hurt Ankylosaurus?
When Ankylosaurus swung its stiffened tail from side to side, the rod of bone supported the tail club and absorbed the shock of it thwacking into a victim.

It probably did this when it just had a thick, bony rod of a tail because even that would hurt—imagine being hit across the legs with a big stick.

Ankylosaurus's stiff tail evolved before its tail club. That's a little bit like getting a handle and then deciding to add an ax head to it.

I am still evolving, don't you know!

When the osteoderms on the tail clumped together to make a club, its weapon got a whole lot fiercer.

WHY DID EPIDENDROSAURUS HAVE A SUPER-LONG FINGER?

No, it wasn't used to pick its nose! It was possibly to dig out insects from trees.

Epidendrosaurus

What was Epidendrosaurus?
Epidendrosaurus was a small, feathered dinosaur, just 12 cm (5 in) long, that lived in China.

What does its name mean?
Its name means "lizard in the tree" and it was well suited to life in the trees.

Is there anything today that's like Epidendrosaurus?
The modern aye-aye, an animal something like a lemur, also has a single super-long finger that it uses for digging insects out of trees. Epidendrosaurus could have done the same.

Long fingers are cool!

Aye-aye

WHICH DINOSAUR SNACKED ON TERMITES?

Albertonykus did. This chicken-sized dinosaur from Alberta, Canada, skittered through the forests 70 million years ago.

What was Albertonykus like?
Albertonykus was a fierce theropod with stumpy little arms and a single big claw suitable for ripping open ant or termite hills.

So, Albertonykus attacked termite hills?
Well, Canada didn't have ant or termite hills. But there is fossilized wood with tunnels probably made by termites. So, paleontologists think that Albertonykus probably broke open rotting wood with its claw and slurped out the termites—not quite the feast of a big termite mound, but a handy snack.

Albertonykus

WHO WAS MAJUNGASAURUS?

Like many other animals that evolved in isolation, Majungasaurus became a little bit odd.

Its fingers probably couldn't even move independently—it was all or nothing for these hands.

Where was Majungasaurus from?
It was a squat and stocky theropod from Madagascar, a large island off the east coast of Africa.

Majungasaurus had strapping shoulders with big bones—but tiny arms.

How about its bite?
It had a wide snout, unlike most theropods—good for biting and holding on if lunch struggled.

Were its fingers any use?
Its tiny stubby fingers probably couldn't grasp anything.

What did Majungasaurus eat?
It was a carnivore and a cannibal—not a cool thing to be.

How do we know it was a cannibal?
Bones of Majungasaurus have been found with tooth marks that match the mouths of Majungasaurus. This is something of a giveaway!

Did it have lots of teeth?
It had more teeth than most dinosaurs of similar types—useful if you want to eat your friends.

It probably couldn't roll its eyes. The part of the brain responsible for quick eye movements was very small.

What else do fossils tell us about Majungasaurus?
Over 20 fossils of Majungasaurus have something wrong with them. This tells us that they weren't very healthy.

WHICH DINOSAUR LOOKS LIKE A MOVIE STAR?

This ankylosaur is named Zuul crurivastator, after a famous character from the silver screen.

What's behind its name?
"Zuul" is named after a monster in the 1984 *Ghostbusters* movie, to whom it bears a striking resemblance. "Crurivastator" means "destroyer of shins" and refers to the giant club of solid bone at the end of Zuul's tail.

When and where did it live?
The dinosaur was found in 2016 in Montana, USA, where it lived 75 million years ago. Despite its fearsome club, it only ate plants.

What did it use its tail for?
To defend itself—it could use its tail to give anything that wanted to eat it a good thwack across the legs.

Zuul crurivastator

Do I get a star on Hollywood Boulevard?

WHAT WAS SPECIAL ABOUT BRACHYTRACHELOPAN?

It was unique among sauropods in having a short neck.

What did it eat?
The dino couldn't reach high-growing leaves, so it probably ate from the ground or from shrubs growing to just 1–2 m (40–80 in) tall.

How did Brachytrachelopan compare to other sauropods?
Compared to its body size, Brachytrachelopan's neck was 40 percent shorter than that of other sauropods—nearly half their length.

Just a short neck?
Brachytrachelopan was also quite stumpy for a sauropod, growing to only 10 m (33 ft).

Brachytrachelopan

Why did it have a short neck?
It might have adapted to a particular type of plant. Its short neck limited the food it could reach, and that might in turn have limited the size it grew to.

Size isn't everything, you know!

WHAT DID RAPTORS EAT?

Fierce raptors like Utahraptor and Deinonychus probably ran over the plains attacking any hapless animal they came across.

What were their teeth like?
They had serrated teeth that were great for slicing into meat. Raptors with these teeth lived in the northern hemisphere, in places such as North America and Mongolia.

What about raptors in the south?
Raptors in the southern hemisphere, like the chicken-sized Buitreraptor and huge Austroraptor in South America, had different teeth. They were smaller, and they had more of them, with no serrations. Instead, they had grooves running along each tooth.

What were these teeth good for?
These teeth were great for snatching fish. Perhaps these raptors stood by riverbanks and ate fish.

Austroraptor

COULD RAPTORS CLIMB TREES?

Yes, though they didn't all do so, because some lived in places without trees.

Did Velociraptor actually climb?
Velociraptor lived in the desert, so it probably missed out on tree climbing.

Was it possible for Velociraptor to climb?
Studies of the giant claw of Velociraptor, thought to be used for holding down prey, show that it was strong enough to support the animal's weight if used to anchor it in a surface—such as tree bark.
If the same was true of other raptor claws, raptors could have scrambled up trees.

Going up!

Why did raptors climb?
Maybe they dropped from above onto their prey. Or maybe it was a step toward flying—or just for fun.

DID SMALL MAMMALS GET STEPPED ON?

Small mammals tried to keep out of the way of dinosaur feet.

Why did mammals burrow?
Not only were dinosaurs big and stompy, many would also snap up a little mammal as a snack, given the chance. One way of keeping out of the way was to dig an underground burrow.

Did this keep mammals safe?
Fossils in Utah show that about 80 million years ago, a dinosaur like a Deinonychus or Troodon used the claws of its back feet to dig into the burrows of small mammals.

Time for lunch, guys!

Scratch marks and burrows are found horrifyingly close together. There was no escape, even underground, from those ruthless predators.

Troodon

WHY ARE TWO CORYTHOSAURUSES AT THE BOTTOM OF THE SEA?

They were the victims of a shipwreck. In 1916, a British ship was crossing the Atlantic Ocean carrying the fossils—a dangerous undertaking during World War I.

What happened to the fossils?
Mount Temple was attacked by an enemy German ship, the passengers and crew were taken off, and then it was sunk with its cargo of fossils.

Corythosaurus

What was Corythosaurus?
Corythosaurus was a plant-eater from Alberta, Canada, that lived 75 million years ago.

What does its name mean?
Its name means "Corinthian-helmet lizard"—it's named after the bony crest that tops its head and looks like a helmet.

What was Corythosaurus's crest used for?
Computer models show that the "helmet" had tubes inside that could make loud, booming sounds as air went through them.

WHICH DINOSAUR CHANGED SCIENTISTS' MINDS?

Deinonychus changed how people thought about dinosaurs—it was the first hint that they might be fast-moving and perhaps warm-blooded. It led people to realize that birds are modern dinosaurs.

How big was Deinonychus?
A full-grown adult was 3.4 m (11 ft) long—as big as an alligator.

How did Deinonychus move?
Deinonychus flapped its wings to help it balance while eating struggling prey.

A stiffened tail helped it to balance, too.

When was Deinonychus alive?
It lived 115–108 million years ago in the western United States.

Was Deinonychus fast?
It could run at up to 56 km/h (35 mph).

Were Diononychus good parents?
Deinonychus parents probably sat on their eggs to keep them warm.

Did Deinonychus have strong jaws?
Its teeth and jaws were strong enough to bite through bone.

What was its "terrible claw" like?
Its long, hinged claw on each back foot would have been covered with a horny sheath, making it even longer: 12 cm (4.7 in).

How big was Coelophysis?

Although it was as tall as a human teenager, it only weighed as much as a small human child at 22.5 kg (50 lb). It was longer than a human teenager, though, at 2.5 m (8 ft) long. Its hollow bones helped to keep it light and nimble.

You've got some growing up to do, kid.

Coelophysis

WHICH DINOSAUR WAS TEENAGER-SIZED?

Coelophysis was. This early dinosaur from about 215 million years ago, was a speedy meat-eater.

What was special about Coelophysis?

Coelophysis was one of the first dinosaurs to evolve a wishbone, the forked bone made of two fused collarbones that birds still have. It had large eyes, so it might have been nocturnal.

Did Coelophysis live in groups?

Thousands of fossils of Coelophysis have been found together in New Mexico, suggesting that they might have lived in herds or packs.

Stegoceras

What was Stegoceras like?

It was a pachycephalosaur, which means it had a thick dome of bone on top of its head like the more famous Pachycephalosaurus.

WAS STEGOCERAS LIKE STEGOSAURUS?

Not at all. While everyone knows what Stegosaurus looked like, Stegoceras is not as famous.

Did all pachycephalosaurs have bumpy heads?

Some had head bumps and some didn't, leading paleontologists to think that males used their bony heads to crash into each other when fighting over mates or territory.

Pachycephalosaurus

No need for a crash helmet!

How big was Stegoceras?

It was just 2–2.5 m (6.6–8.2 ft) long and weighed up to about 40 kg (88 lb).

Did Stegoceras use its crown to headbutt?

About a fifth of fossils with head bumps also have head injuries.

Was it two-legged or four-legged?

It ran around on two legs in the North American forests 75 million years ago.

WHICH DINO WAS THE ONLY MEAT-EATER WITH HORNS?

Carnotaurus, whose name means "meat-eating bull." It sounds pretty freaky. Adding horns makes it no better.

How long were Carnotaurus's horns?
In its fossils, Carnotaurus's horns are bony stumps just 15 cm (6 in).

In life, they might have been topped with much longer keratin horns.

Where did Carnotaurus live?
Carnotaurus lived in Argentina 72–70 million years ago and was as long as a truck at 7.5 m (24.5 ft) long.

What else was different about Carnotaurus?
As well as the horns, it had little bony lumps called osteoderms over its back and sides.

WAS VELOCIRAPTOR A GIANT?

It got a bad reputation as mean and fierce from the Jurassic Park movies, but Velociraptor was only the size of a turkey at about 60 cm (2 ft) tall. And it was feathery, too, which doesn't sound so scary.

Would a Velociraptor attack be dangerous?
Being attacked by Velociraptor would have been more like a fight with an angry chicken with teeth, or a smallish dog than a deadly battle with a crocodile or a tiger.

Hey, I'm no turkey!

Were the movie Velociraptors wrong?
The Velociraptors in the Jurassic Park movies were actually based on a different, bigger dinosaur called Deinonychus. Deinonychus weighed about seven times as much as a Velociraptor and lived 30 million years earlier.

WERE TRICERATOPS FIGHTERS?

Triceratops

The horns on a Triceratops were pretty sharp and could have been used to try and fight off a predator. But that's not all they were for.

I'm ready for battle!

How do we know that Triceratops fought?
Some Triceratops fossils have evidence of injuries around the frill that match Triceratops horns. That suggests they locked horns in fights with each other.

Monoceratops

Pick on your own type!

Many horned animals today use their horns in battles over mates or territory. It seems that Triceratops might well have done the same.

Did Triceratops fight Monoceratops?
Monoceratops fossils don't have the long brow horns and don't have the same injuries, so it looks like Triceratops kept its squabbles to its own kind.

WHICH DINO BLEW ITS OWN TRUMPET?

Parasaurolophus had a trumpet-like bony head crest that curved backward and could be 1.5 m (5 ft) long.

A cross section of Parasaurolophus's crest appears to show four tubes, but it's really two that loop around at the top end and finish at each nostril.

What did it sound like?
Inside, passages and tubes carried air around, producing a noise on the out breath like a krummhorn.

Parasaurolophus

Why would Parasaurolophus make a trumpeting sound?
Parasaurolophus probably trumpeted to communicate with each other through the forest, their low-frequency sounds carrying over a long distance.

When was Parasaurolophus around?
Parasaurolophus lived 76.5–73 million years ago in North America.

How did Regaliceratops get its nickname?

It was nicknamed "Hellboy" by paleontologists because its short brow horns reminded them of a character in a graphic novel who had short horns growing from his forehead.

How showy was Regaliceratops?

Regaliceratops is one of the fancier types of ceratopsian dinosaurs. What it lacks in size of horns, it makes up for in numbers with a total of 15 horns arranged around its frill, as well as two above its eyes and a nose horn. That makes an extravagant total of 18 horns!

What does its name mean?

Its real name means "royal horned face," referring to the way its arrangement of horns looks like a crown.

WHICH DINO WAS NAMED AFTER A COMIC CHARACTER?

Regaliceratops, or "Hellboy," lived in Canada 68 million years ago. It was discovered in 2015.

Regaliceratops

DO WE KNOW WHAT DINO SKIN LOOKED LIKE?

Paleontologists can use information about modern animals to help them discover what dinosaurs looked like—not just whether they were big or small, but even whether they were green or brown.

How do we know about Psittacosaurus's skin pattern?

After a very well-preserved fossil of Psittacosaurus was found in China, scientists could figure out the pigments in its skin. From this, they could build a model of the dinosaur using the right shades of brown, black, and yellow, then try it out in different kinds of lighting to figure out where it lived.

How was its patterning useful?

Its patterning is best suited to being hidden in the dappled overhead light of a forest.

We're hard to spot!

Psittacosaurus

HOW SMART WAS STEGOSAURUS?

Not very. Stegosaurus had a funny-shaped skull, like a tube or a banana. There was only space inside for a brain the size of a walnut.

In 1920, one dinosaur enthusiast suggested that Stegosaurus used its scutes to fly. It didn't.

Early dinosaur experts thought that Stegosaurus walked on two legs. It didn't do that, either.

What does the name "Stegosaurus" mean?
Its name means "roof lizard." Early on, people thought its scutes (plates) lay flat, like roof tiles

Did all Stegosaurus have the same number of tail spikes?
Different stegosaur species had different numbers of spikes, from four to ten.

How long were the tail spikes?
The spikes could be up to 90 cm (3 ft) long.

Did Stegosarus have cheeks?
Yes. Stegosaurus was one of the first dinosaurs to evolve cheeks.

Where did Stegosaurus live?
More stegosaurs came from Asia than from North America, though Stegosaurus is one of the most famous American dinosaurs.

Why should you never walk behind a Stegosaurus?
The animal could swipe its tail from side to side quickly, delivering a dangerous thwack.

The arrangement of bony spikes on the end of its tail is unofficially called a "thagomizer." The name comes from a cartoon drawn by Gary Larson in 1982.

WHO FOUND AN ICHTHYOSAUR AT THE AGE OF 12?

Mary Anning. She was the first great fossil hunter, active in England in the early 1800s from her childhood.

In 1811, her older brother found an ichthyosaur skull and, the following year Mary found the rest of the animal. They had both learned fossil hunting with their father, and after his death she supported the family by finding and selling fossils.

Throw me a bone!

Ichthyosaur skull

Where did Mary learn about fossils?
Mary left school young, but taught herself so much about fossils that she knew more than the professional scientists.

What else did Mary find?
She found the first Plesiosaurus as well as a large number of ichthyosaur fossils. She went fossil hunting with her dog, Tray, along the coast of Dorset, dodging rock falls and dangerous tides.

WAS MAIASAURA A GOOD PARENT?

We think so. Maiasaura laid 30–40 eggs at a time and seem to have cared for their babies after they hatched.

How do we know that Maiasaura looked after its young?
A giant fossilized nesting site, where many Maiasaura parents made their nests, preserves babies that died near the nests, suggesting that they were cared for as they grew.

What does Maiasaura mean?
The name Maiasaura means "good mother reptile." Maiasaura covered the nest with vegetation, which kept the eggs warm as it rotted. Since the parents each weighed about 5 tons, it was safer than sitting on them!

How big were Maiasaura eggs?
The eggs were 15 cm (6 in) long, and the babies grew more than 90 cm (3 ft) in their first year.

Tratayenia

Can you guess what I look like, guys?

WHAT DID TRATAYENIA LOOK LIKE?

Terrifying! This mega-raptor, discovered in South America in 2006, was hunting prey 95–85 million years ago.

How hard was it to figure out what Tratayenia looked like?

Tratayenia is a triumph of dinosaur scientists' skills. Although they have found only some hip and back bones, they can piece together what the dino looked like, and figure out its size by comparing it with similar types of mega-big raptors (called megaraptorids).

How big was Tratayenia?

Tratayenia was 9 m (30 ft) long and probably had giant, meathook claws that grew up to 40 cm (16 in).

WHOSE FOSSIL GOT BLOWN TO BITS?

The huge Italian Jurassic meat-eater, Saltriovenator.

When the mountain range of the Alps was pushed up 30 million years ago, Saltriovenator was carried with them.

How did the fossil get blown up?

It had the misfortune to be buried in what became a marble quarry, and it was blasted to bits with dynamite by miners.

Where was it found?

There is a single fossil, which was found in the Italian Alps—but it had taken a few knocks.

My luck must change soon ...

What did the bones show?

They showed the marks of the dead dino that had been eaten by marine animals after it died. What was left was fossilized under the sea.

Saltriovenator

77

DOES EVERY T. REX HAVE A NAME?

All the recent major T. rex fossils do.
No other type of dinosaur
gets such special treatment.

What do T. rexes get named?
The named T. rex fossils are: Stan, Wankel, Sue, Scotty, Bucky, Jane, Thomas, Tristan, Baby Bob, Trix, and Tufts-Love.

Where are these T. rexes?
Most are in the USA, but Scotty is in Canada, Trix in the Netherlands, and Tristan's new home is in Germany.

When did we start naming T. rexes?
No T. rexes were found between 1908 and 1987. All those found since 1987 have been named—we've learned how to treat our T. rexes properly.

> Tonight, we have Stan on drums and Sue on guitar!

WHICH DINO HAD BAD REVIEWS?

Dilophosaurus is possibly the most misunderstood of all dinosaurs.

How did Dilophosaurus appear in the movies?
It appeared in the first Jurassic Park movie in 1993 as a poison-spitting, frill-wiggling animal the size of a Labrador. But Dilophosaurus was awesome in its own ways, not the ways of a director's imagination.

> I'm not toxic— I'm cool!

Did Dilophosaurus spit poison?
No. And it didn't have a frill that could expand either. And also, it was much bigger than a dog. Its name was hijacked for something that doesn't exist.

What was Dilophosaurus really like?
Dilophosaurus had a perfectly respectable double head crest, was 6.5 m (20 ft) long, and weighed more than a large bear.

How was Dilophosaurus a pioneer?
It's unusual as an early Jurassic dinosaur from North America. Dinosaurs had only recently arrived there from South America, so early specimens are rare.

ARE VELOCIRAPTORS LIKE THEIR MOVIE VERSION?

The Velociraptors in Jurassic Park are much closer to Deinonychus than to real Velociraptors.

Did Velociraptor hunt in packs?
Velociraptor fossils have only been found alone, so there is no evidence that they hunted in packs or lived in groups.

Was Velociraptor fast?
The name "Velociraptor" means "speedy thief." It could probably manage 40 km/h (25 mph) in short bursts.

Was Velociraptor scaly?
Velociraptor had feathers, not scales.

How large was Velociraptor?
It was about the height of a large chicken—but more fierce. And with a longer tail.

It would take around seven real Velociraptors to make something the size of a Jurassic Park Velociraptor, if you could melt them down and combine them.

Was Velociraptor smart?
Although it was pretty smart for a dinosaur, Velociraptor was not smart enough to figure out how to use a door knob, as it does in the movie.

What prey did Velociraptor hunt?
Far from attacking a child (had there been any), Velociraptor probably hunted only small prey.

WHICH DINOSAUR HAD THE WACKIEST HORNS?

Machairoceratops was a ceratopsian dinosaur from North America. It didn't invest much in its frill, but it must win a prize for its horns.

What were its horns like?
Two huge, curving, sickle-like horns came from the top of its frill and bent down over its face. The "machairis" part of its name means "bent sword."

I'm not the weird one...

Machairoceratops

Did it have a horny nose?
Machairoceratops had no nose horn, but it had two big brow horns. Then, its somewhat stunted frill swept up into another couple of horns that gave it a pretty spiky front end.

Was it a large dinosaur?
It wasn't the largest of the ceratopsian dinosaurs, at 6–8 m (20–26 ft) long. It weighed only half as much as a Triceratops—but it was one of the most spectacular.

WHO WAS KING OF THE DINOS BEFORE T. REX?

Allosaurus was the T. rex of its era.

How tough was Allosaurus?
This chunky meat-eater could take down a medium-sized sauropod, and had fights with Stegosaurus (it didn't always win).

Was Allosaurus fast?
It could run 34 km/h (21 mph), which isn't superfast, but it was fast enough to catch its dinner.

Hiding won't help...

Did Allosaurus and T. rex meet?
Allosaurus lived 155 million years ago (so we're closer in time to T. rex than Allosaurus was), but there was little getting away from it—fossils have been found as far apart as North America, Portugal, Siberia, and Thailand.

Allosaurus

WHICH DINOSAUR GOT TURNED INTO A TATTOO?

Wendiceratops. Wendy Sloboda, who discovered the fossil in 2011, had the dino tattooed on her arm.

Wendiceratops

Wendiceratops lived in Canada 79 million years ago and was a smaller early cousin of Triceratops.

What was Wendiceratops like?
It had a blunt nose horn, two brow horns, and little curled spikes around the edge of its frill. You might have thought it more cute than threatening if it weren't for the big horns over its eyes.

I am art!

WHICH DINOSAUR HID IN A CUPBOARD FOR 80 YEARS?

Rativates first hid underground for 75 million years. Then, when it was dug up, this dino fossil was wrongly classified and left in storage.

In 2016, paleontologists dug this forgotten fossil out of the cupboard and had a good look, discovering that it was a new species.

What was it like?
Rativates was an ornithomimid, which means it looked like a bird, and it is ostrich-like—except for the long tail.

What does its name mean?
Its full name, *Rativates evadens*, refers to its ability to evade detection for such a long time.

Rativates

How big was it?
It was probably 3 m (10 ft) long, including the tail, and about 1.5 m (5 ft) tall.

DID T. REX HAVE FEATHERS?

The adult didn't, but T. rex babies might have had feathery fluff.

What was T. rex's skin like?
Fossils show T. rex had scaly, reptilian skin, just as it has always been imagined.

Why didn't T. rex have feathers?
If T. rex had had feathers, it would probably have overheated. For the same reason, the giant mammals of Africa, like elephants and rhinos, don't have furry bodies.

Were there any feathery T. rex look-alikes?
Its Chinese relative Yutyrannus was close in size to T. rex, and had filament-like feathers. While T. rex spent its life in the hot environment of western North America, Yutyrannus lived in a colder climate. Feathers would have been good to keep it warm.

Earlier wool-coated rhinos and mammoths lived in cold areas and needed help keeping warm.

My fluffy babies!

WHO NAMED THE MOST DINOSAURS?

Othniel Marsh. He was a human dino star, one of the greatest American fossil hunters of the late 1800s.

How did Marsh get started?
A rich uncle died and left him US $100,000, which he used to set up a fossil hunting empire. He employed a large number of people to find fossils, which he then studied and named.

No one leaves Triceratops in storage!

How many fossils did he find?
In all, Marsh and his workers found more than 500 fossilized animals, including the first American pterosaurs and some of the most famous dinosaurs, such as Stegosaurus, Triceratops, Brontosaurus, and Allosaurus. He named 80 species of dinosaur.

Did he study them all?
Marsh collected so many fossils that he could not possibly have studied them all. Many lay in storage for decades, unexamined.

WHO WAS MARSH'S GREATEST RIVAL?

Edward Drinker Cope tried to claim Marsh's crown.

... 999, and 1,000!

Camarasaurus

Dimetrodon

What did he discover?
Among the animals he discovered were Coelophysis, Camarasaurus, and the pre-dinosaurian reptile, Dimetrodon.

His rivalry with Marsh (see page 82) involved some very odd practices, but he achieved a lot. He published 1,400 scientific papers in his life.

How many dinosaurs did he name?
Although he had little formal education, Cope named 56 new American dinosaurs in the 1900s—1,000 prehistoric animals overall.

Did Cope go too far?
Eventually, his passion for dinosaur hunting and his rivalry with Marsh led to him run out of money.

WHAT'S THE CONNECTION BETWEEN T. REX AND THE CIRCUS?

Barnum Brown, who named T. rex, was named after a famous circus showman, P.T. Barnum. He was an eccentric individual, often turning up to fossil digs wearing a long beaver-fur coat, and always wearing a tie.

Was Brown a fossil hunter?
Brown was one of the greatest fossil hunters of the 1900s. He found plenty of other animals besides dinosaurs.

Where did Brown explore?
He was employed by the American Museum of Natural History to hunt for and acquire fossils in North America. He spent several years floating down a river in Canada on a flatboat, stopping at any site that looked as though it might yield fossils.

What was his biggest find?
He found his T. rex in 1902.

WHICH DINOS ARE RECORD BREAKERS?

Mamenchisaurus

Who had the longest neck?
Mamenchisaurus had the longest neck of any dinosaur. It was 9 m (30 ft) or more.

Whose tail was three times its body length?
Leaellynasaura's tail was three times the length of the dinosaur's body—the longest body:tail ratio of any dinosaur.

Which dino was named Sue?
A T. rex fossil. It was found by Sue Hendrickson in 1990 and was named after her.

Who was the most frilling dinosaur?
Kosmoceratops had the largest frill of any ceratopsian dinosaur.

I wasn't named Sue when I was alive!

Leaellynasaura

Who was top for teeth?
Pelecanimimus had more teeth than any other meat-eater, about 220.

Spinosaurus

Who had the longest tail?
The sauropod Maraapunisaurus had possibly the longest tail ever, at around 30 m (98 ft). Another estimate makes the dino only half as long. There are no complete fossils, so it's hard to tell.

Who was the largest meat-eater?
Spinosaurus was the largest meat-eater at 15 m (50 ft) long.

Who laid the biggest eggs?
Hypselosaurus laid the biggest-known egg of any dinosaur. It was 30 cm (12 in) long and could contain about 73 chicken eggs.

Who were the biggest raptors?
Austroraptor and Utahraptor are the largest-known raptors, at 6.4 m (21 ft) long—big and scary!

Pachycephalosaurus wyomingensis

Who has the thickest skull?
Pachycephalosaurus wyomingensis had the thickest skull, at 40 cm (16 in).

Utahraptor

WHICH DINOSAUR WAS CLUB BOSS?

Although Ankylosaurus is the most famous ankylosaur, Anodontosaurus had a more impressive tail club.

Anodontosaurus

Want to go clubbing? I'm ready!

What was Anodontosaurus's tail club like?
Anodontosaurus had a much wider and sassier tail club than Ankylosaurus's spoon-shaped club

What does Anodontosaurus's name mean?
Poor Anodontosaurus's name means "toothless lizard," though it wasn't toothless at all.

How much bad luck did Anodontosaurus's fossil suffer?
The head of the first fossil found had suffered damage over the 70 million years it had spent in the ground, and the teeth were gone.

It had more bad luck, too—scientists decided for a time that it wasn't a separate type of dino at all, but just the same as Euoplocephalus. It got its name back in 2010, though.

HOW WAS BARYONYX DISCOVERED?

The British dinosaur Baryonyx was found in 1983 when fossil hunter William Walker saw a bit of claw sticking out of the ground.

Fish, fowl, Iguanodon ... I'm not fussy

How did it hunt?
It probably stood in the shallows and hunted fish—but the remains of an Iguanodon in one dino's stomach area suggests that it wasn't too fussy to eat something else if it came along.

Baryonyx

What did the claw turn out to be?
It was a huge, curved talon 31 cm (12.5 in) long. The rest of the dinosaur was behind it, too.

What was Baryonyx like?
Baryonyx lived 125 million years ago in what were then the hot swamps of southern England. Its nostrils were set high on its nose, and it had a crocodile-like mouth with curved, spiny teeth, perfect for catching fish.

WHAT WAS THE FIRST SAUROPOD TO BE FOUND?

CETIOSAURUS. HOWEVER, IT WASN'T RECOGNIZED AS A SAUROPOD AT THE TIME.

Not a sauropod? How dare you!

What does Cetiosaurus mean?
It means "whale lizard." The name was chosen because Richard Owen, the man who first described it in 1842, thought it was some kind of marine animal, perhaps like a crocodile.

Was Cetiosaurus a giant?
It was quite small for a sauropod at just 16 m (52 ft), and weighed only 11,000 kg (12 tons)—which is a lot for anything else, but not for a sauropod.

Where did Cetiosaurus live?
Although most sauropods are found in North and South America, Cetiosaurus lived in Europe 167 million years ago and was first found in England.

WHICH DINOSAUR SNACKED ON WORMS?

Usually considered a plant-eating dinosaur, Ankylosaurus may have also eaten grubs.

Yum! Yum! Yum!

Did Ankylosaurus fart?
Yes. It had no chewing teeth, and a big, round belly. The leaves it ate would have gone straight to the belly, where bacteria would have fermented them (making the ankylosaur a pretty gassy animal).

Did it only eat plants?
Recently scientists have suggested that Ankylosaurus might also have rooted in the soil for grubs, bugs, worms, and perhaps roots.

Does its nose provide any clues about the Ankylosaurus diet?
Its nostrils are set on top of its head, which is common for animals that stick their nose in the dirt. That's sensible—no one wants nostrils full of mud.

Could Ankylosaurus dig?
Its front feet were strong enough for digging, and it had a good sense of smell, which would have helped it find food underground.

WHOSE DINO DROPPINGS ARE OFF THE SCALE?

A fossilized T. rex dropping found in Canada in 1998 is 45 cm (1.5 ft) long. That's pretty big.

Quick! Run! I just did a really big, smelly poop!

T. rex

How did scientists know the poop came from T. rex?
They came up with T. rex as the only large-enough meat-eater that could crunch up bone.

What was in the T. rex poop?
The dino dropping had quite a lot of undigested soft tissue in it, which tells us that T. rex wolfed down its meal in big gulps, and then the food didn't stay in its gut for very long before coming out the other end.

How do scientists identify dinosaur poop?
Dino droppings don't come with a label explaining which animal they are from. Scientists have to figure it out from the kind of food it contains and the animals that would have been around millions of years ago when it was dropped.

WHICH DINOSAUR WAS THE FANCIEST FRILLER?

There are a good number of contenders for the title "frilliest frill" among the ceratopsian dinosaurs. Kosmoceratops probably wins.

Kosmoceratops

How big was Kosmoceratops's frill?
Its skull, including both head and the bony shield that formed the frill, was 2 m (6.5 ft) long.

The massive frill had 15 small horns curving inward, so it looked floppy rather than frightening.

Where did Kosmoceratops live?
Kosmoceratops lived in the hot swamps of the western part of North America 76 million years ago, before its later cousin, Triceratops. It was a good, lush area nicknamed the "lost continent" by fossil hunters.

I'll give you "frilliest frill"!

WHICH DINO PAIR SHARED A THUMB SPIKE?

Two barely related dinosaurs from Mongolia both had a nose hump and a thumb spike.

Both Choyrodon and the larger Altirhinus were types of iguanodont dinosaur (like Iguanodon), but developed their nose-humps separately and in different ways.

Choyrodon

What was the nose hump made of?
The nose hump seems to have been squishy flesh attached to a raised nose ridge of bone.

Don't squish it!

What use was a nose-hump?
It might have been part of the dino's way of looking attractive to a mate. Perhaps it was bright and eye-catching, or maybe it could make a noise—but we really don't know.

WHICH DINOSAUR HAD A WONKY BACK?

Stegosaurus. The plates along its back were arranged in an odd way.

What was Stegosaurus missing?
Stegosaurus also missed out on giant shoulder spikes, which most other types of stegosaurs had.

How were stegosaur spikes useful?
They made it hard for a predator to get too close to the front of stegosaurs. But spikes would also have made the stegosaurs unwieldy, giving them problems squeezing between bushes and trees.

Stegosaurus

Why were Stegosaurus's plates odd?
Most stegosaurs had spikes or plates arranged in neat symmetrical rows, but the plates that run from the back of a Stegosaurus neck to its tail are in an odd, asymmetric arrangement. No one knows why, or how this might have helped Stegosaurus.

Not being eaten was worth a little hassle in tight places.

Who are you calling wonky?

WAS SPINOSAURUS BIGGER THAN T. REX?

Spinosaurus was the largest meat-eating dinosaur—even bigger than T. rex and Allosaurus.

How big?
It grew to 12.5–18 m (41–59 ft) long and weighed up to 18,000 kg (20 tons).

Where did it live?
It lived in North Africa 112–97 million years ago.

How long were its spines?
A row of spines along its back were up to 1.6 m (5.4 ft) long.

When was Spinosaurus discovered?
The first fossil of Spinosaurus was discovered in Egypt in 1915.

Do we still have the first Spinosaurus fossil?
No. That fossil was destroyed in a bombing raid on Munich, Germany, in World War II.

Luckily, another was found in Morocco in 2014.

Come on in—the water's lovely!

What did the spines look like?
They might have supported a hump or a sail. It's usually drawn with a sail.

What did Spinosaurus eat?
Spinosaurus ate fish. It had a crocodile-like snout and curved, sharp teeth to keep fish from slipping out of its mouth.

Did Spinosaurus go swimming for food?
Spinosaurus could have caught fish while wading in shallow water or swimming. It was too light to dive for food, and would have bobbed up to the surface!

WHICH DINO WAS NAMED AFTER A SHARK?

Carcharodontosaurus's name means, "Great White Shark lizard" and it was worthy of the name.

How big was Carcharodontosaurus?

Not quite as big as T. rex, Carcharodontosaurus was probably 12 m (40 ft) long—big enough to be scary. It lived in Africa alongside Spinosaurus.

Did it have teeth like a shark?

The teeth that give Carcharodontosaurus its name were 16 cm (6 in) long, serrated, and looked like curved steak knives.

Did Carcharodontosaurus have a big head?

For a long time, scientists only had teeth to work with because the first large fossil of Carcharodontosaurus was destroyed by bombs in World War II. Another skull discovered in 1995 confirmed its fearsome size—the skull alone is 1.5 m (5.2 ft) long.

Don't call me Jaws!

Carcharodontosaurus

DID CROCODILES LIVE WITH DINOSAURS?

The crocodile-like Sarcosuchus terrorized snack-sized dinosaurs of Africa 112 million years ago.

Was Sarcosuchus a fast grower?

It took 40–50 years to grow to adult size—so at 30, it was still a teenager!

Was Sarcosuchus a giant?

The biggest of crocodile-like animals, it grew to 12 m (39 ft)—twice the length of the largest modern crocodile, the saltwater crocodile.

Was it a fish-eater?

The style of its teeth suggests that Sarcosuchus didn't focus on fish for its dinner but was a generalist, snapping up any hapless creature that came near. That would include dinosaurs.

I'm not a fussy eater!

Sarcosuchus

WHICH DINOSAUR HAD A SPIKY NECKLACE?

Sauropelta was a spiny-necked North American nodosaur (a relative of the ankylosaurs).

Sauropelta

Were neck spikes useful?
Sauropelta ate low-growing plants, so it would have spent its time with its head down on the ground.

It had huge spikes on the back of its neck, which faced upward and backward. And then it had a row of smaller spikes that stuck out at the side.

Any predator coming from the front would have seen a bristling collection of spikes. It would probably have gone off to look for an easier meal!

WHO WAS THE AMERICAS' BIGGEST TERROR?

T. rex was big and fearsome, but Giganotosaurus was bigger—one of the biggest theropod dinosaurs ever. Only Spinosaurus was bigger.

Giganotosaurus

Argentinosaurus

Was Giganotosaurus scary?
Giganotosaurus was big and ferocious with huge, blade-like teeth. It could run reasonably fast.

Could Giganotosaurus prey on a titanosaur?
It was so awesome that a group of Giganotosauruses could probably bring down huge titanosaurs like Argentinosaurus.

When was Giganotosaurus around?
Giganotosaurus lived around 100–97 million years ago in South America. It was more closely related to Carcharodontosaurus in Africa than to the later T. rex in North America.

WHICH DINOSAUR WAS SHIP-SHAPED?

When dinosaur hunters found jaws of a new type of dinosaur in Australia, the shape reminded them of the upturned hull of a galleon, an ancient type of boat. So they called the new dinosaur Galleonosaurus.

Galleonosaurus jaw

Did Galleonosaurus live in a herd?

As five were found together, they probably lived in social groups.

Was Galleonosaurus ship-sized?

Galleonosaurus lived 125 million years ago and was about as big as a wallaby—small for a dinosaur, and even smaller for a ship! It would have scampered around eating plants.

It's similar to some dinosaurs found in South America, showing again that dinosaurs trekked across Antarctica.

Galleonosaurus

hull

upturned galleon

DOES SUPERSAURUS DESERVE ITS NAME?

You'd think a dinosaur named Supersaurus would have to be the biggest, the fastest, the coolest, or the something-est.

I'm super!

But no. Supersaurus was a fairly middle-of-the-road kind of sauropod.

Was Supersaurus the heaviest?

It lived in North America in the Jurassic, just like many others. It weighed about 40 tons, which is fairly big, but by no means the heaviest sauropod.

Was Supersaurus the longest?

It was extremely long at around 33.5 m (110 ft), but that still isn't the longest of all—Argentinosaurus could be 39 m (130 ft) long. It's a little risky giving a dinosaur a name like Supersaurus because you never know what else might turn up later …

DID HEAVY DINOSAURS SQUASH THEIR EGGS?

Some dinosaurs laid eggs in nests, but if a heavy dinosaur sat on its eggs, they'd soon be scrambled!

How did dinosaurs avoid cracking their eggs?
Some big dinosaurs laid the eggs in a ring and sat in the middle. Some didn't sit on them at all, but kept them warm with plant matter.

Did the eggs stay warm?
The eggs stayed warm enough and safe, but they weren't crushed by the parent's weight.

What were dinosaur nests like?
Fossilized nests sometimes have a space in the middle of the eggs for a big, hefty dinosaur to sit. Beibeilong, in China, looked like a modern cassowary—a giant bird with a bony crest. It was 8 m (26 ft) long and made a nest 2.5 m (8 ft) across with around 24 eggs arranged in a circle.

DID ANY DINOSAUR HAVE 1,000 TEETH?

Dinos like Hadrosaurus had a toothless beak at the front of the mouth, but well-stocked tooth "batteries" at the back that had up to 1,000 teeth. And they were pretty odd teeth.

Hadrosaurus skull

What were hadrosaur teeth like?
Hadrosaur teeth were closely packed, with no gaps between them, looking something like a huge super-tooth.

How were hadrosaur teeth different to human teeth?
Unlike your teeth, which have a soft, pulpy part inside, Hadrosaur teeth had died and turned solid before they came through the gum. The hadrosaur could wear them down by grinding its food, and it didn't hurt.

Why were hadrosaur teeth like this?
The hadrosaur needed to grind because it fed on conifers (fir trees) that have tough, spiky needles.

Lots of work for the tooth fairy!

WHAT WAS THE FIRST-KNOWN DINOSAUR?

Iguanodon is a dino-star for kick-starting the whole dinosaur thing.

I'm Number One!

Who gave dinosaurs their name?

Seeing parts of Iguanodon and two other dinosaur fossils led the British geologist Richard Owen to propose that there had been extinct large animals, which he named "dinosaurs."

What was Iguanodon mistaken for?

When Mary and Gideon Mantell showed Iguanodon teeth to the French expert, Georges Cuvier, he thought they came from something like a large pufferfish.

Then he suggested a large, extinct, plant-eating reptile of some kind. Mantell looked in museums and saw an iguana skeleton. He named the fossil he and his wife had found "Iguanodon."

The next suggestion was a kind of reptile-rhino with a horn on its nose. The horn was identified as a thumb spike in the 1870s.

HOW DO WE KNOW WHAT HAPPENED JUST AFTER THE ASTEROID STRUCK?

In 2019, paleontologists found a fossil field in North Dakota, USA, that preserves the moments after the deadly asteroid struck the Gulf of Mexico 66 million years ago.

What was found on the fossil site?

The area is littered with the fossils of animals killed instantly, including fish hurled ashore by a vast tsunami (wave), their bodies and gills studded with fragments of rock.

Tiny blobs of scalding rock rained from the sky and started fires where they fell on land. They are found as balls of rock all over the site and embedded in animal bodies.

Did the dinos die when the asteroid hit?

The moment of catastrophe at this site, 3,000 km (1,865 miles) away from the Gulf of Mexico, would have come 40 minutes after the impact.

HOW DID THE DINOSAURS DIE OUT?

Dust and smoke darkened the sky, making it colder, possibly for years.

There might have been more than one impact— some asteroids break up as they enter a planet's atmosphere.

A heat pulse from the crash might have killed and even cooked animals.

The asteroid landed in the sea. It would have created waves 100–300 m (325–1,000 ft) high.

Acid rain would have killed even more trees, leaving plant-eaters hungry.

Scalding winds from the impact would have started wildfires.

Waves flooded North and South America, ripping down forests and washing away animals.

Earthquakes caused by the impact killed more plants and animals.

The changes to the climate and landscape were too rapid for animals to adapt— and so they died.

HOW TO SPEAK DINOSAUR

DINO NAME PRONOUNCIATION GUIDE

Albertonykus: **al-BUR-toh-ny-kus**

Allosaurus: **AL-oh-SORE-us**

Altirhinus: **AL-ti-rhy-nus**

Amargosaurus: **ah-MARG-ah-SORE-us**

Anchiornis: **AN-kee-OR-niss**

Anhanguera: **AN-han-GER-a**

Ankylosaurus: **an-KIH-loh-SORE-us**

Anodontosaurus: **an-oh-DONT-oh-SORE-us**

Aquilops: **AK-wihl-opz**

Archaeopteryx: **ARK-ee-OPT-er-ix**

Argentinosaurus: **AR-juhn-TEE-no-SORE-us**

Austroraptor: **aws-troh-rap-tor**

Baryonyx: **BAH-ree-ON-icks**

Beibeilong: **bay-bay-long**

Borealopelta: **bo-ree-oll-pell-ter**

Brachiosaurus: **BRAH-kee-oh-SORE-us**

Brachytrachelopan: **brak-i-trak-eh-loh-pan**

Buitreraptor: **bwee-tree-rap-tor**

Caelestiventus: **See-LES-tih-VEN-təs**

Camarasaurus: **KAM-uh-ruh-SORE-us**

Carcharodontosaurus: **Kar-KAR-o-don-toe-sore-us**

Carnotaurus: **KAR-no-TORE-us**

Cetiosaurus: **see-tee-SORE-us**

Choyrodon: **choy-row-don**

Coelophysis: **see-loh-FISE-iss**

Coelurosauravus: **-SORE-uh-vus**

Compsognathus: **komp-sog-NAY-thus**

Corythosaurus: **KOH-rith-oh-SORE-us**

Deinonychus: **dy-NON-ik-us**

Dilophosaurus: **dy-LOFF-oh-SORE-us**

Diluvicursor: **dy-LOO-vee-KUR-suh**

Dimetrodon: **dy-MET-roh-don**

Dimorphodon: **dy-MOR-foh-don**

Diplodocus: **dip-LOH-doh-kus**

Dracorex: **dray-ko-rex**

Dreadnoughtus: **dred-naw-tus**

Epidendrosaurus: **epi-DEN-droh-SORE-us**

Epidexipteryx: **Epi-decks-ip-ter-iks**

Eudimorphodon: **You-di-mor-fo-don**

Euoplocephalus: **you-OH-plo-KEF-ah-lus**

Euparkeria: **yu-PAR-ker-ree-ah**

Galleonosaurus: **gall-ee-un-oh-SORE-us**

Giganotosaurus: **jig-an-OH-toe-SORE-us**

Hadrosaurus: **HAD-ro-SORE-us**

Halszkaraptor: **halls-car-rap-tor**

Hatzegopteryx: **HAT-zee-GOP-ter-ix**

Henodus: **HEN-oh-duss**

Herrerasaurus: **huh-RARE-uh-SORE-us**

Hesperonychus: **HES-per-on-nee-chuss**

Hylaeosaurus: **HIGH-lee-oh-SORE-us**

Hypselosaurus: **Hip-sel-oh-SORE-us**

Ichthyornis: **ik-thee-ORN-is**

Ichthyosaurus: **ICK-thee-oh-SORE-us**

Iguanodon: **ig-WAH-noh-don**

Koolasuchus: **COOL-ah-SUCH-us**

Kosmoceratops: **cos-mo-SEH-ra-tops**

Leaellynasaura: **LEE-ELL-IN-a-SORE-a**

Lystrosaurus: **liss-tro-SORE-us**

Machairoceratops: **Mak-air--oh-SEH-ra-tops**

Magyarosaurus: **MOD-yar-oh-SORE-us**

Maiasaura: **MY-ah-SORE-ah**

Majungasaurus: **Mah-jung-ah-SORE-us**

Mamenchisaurus: **MAH-men-kee-SORE-us**

Mammoth: **MAM-uth**

Maraapunisaurus: **Ma-rah-pu-ne-SORE-us**

Massospondylus: **mas-oh-SPON-di-lus**

Megalosaurus: **meh-GAH-lo-SORE-us**

Microraptor: **MY-kroh-rap-tuhr**

Monoceratops: **mon-oh-SEH-ra-tops**

Mosasaurus: **MOH-sah-SORE-us**

Mussaurus: **muh-SORE-us**

Nemicolopterus: **NEH-me-co-LOP-ter-us**

Nothosaurus: **NO-tho-SORE-us**

Nothronychus: **noh-thron-i-kus**

Nyasasaurus: **nye-AS-suh-SORE-us**

Nyctosaurus: **NICK-toe-SORE-us**

Oryctodromeus: **oh-RIC-to-DRO-ee-us**

Pachycephalosaurus: **pak-ee-SEF-ah-lo-SORE-us**

Parasaurolophus: **PA-ra-sore-OL-off-us**

Pegomastax: **Pay-go-mah-stax**

Pelecanimimus: **pel-e-kan-i-mim-us**

Placodus: **PLACK-oh-duss**

Plateosaurus: **PLAT-ee-oh-SORE-us**

Plesiosaurus: **PLEH-zee-oh-SORE-us**

Postosuchus: **POST-oh-SOOK-us**

Protoceratops: **PRO-toh-SEH-rah-tops**

Psittacosaurus: **SIT-ak-oh-SORE-us**

Pterodactylus: **TEH-ro-DACK-tih-lus**

Quetzalcoatlus: **KWETS-ul-koh-AT-lus**

Rajasaurus: **ra-ja-SORE-us**

Rativates: **rat-ah-vay-tes**

Regaliceratops: **Ree-gal-li-SEH-ra-tops**

Saltriovenator: **sal-tree-oh-ve-nay-tor**

Sarcosuchus: **sahr-koh-SOOK-us**

Sauropelta: **sore-oh-pelt-ah**

Sciurumimus: **SHOE-ruh-MIME-us**

Sinosauropteryx: **SIGH-no-sore-OP-tuh-rix**

Spinosaurus: **SPINE-oh-SORE-us**

Stegoceras: **ste-GOS-er-as**

Stegosaurus: **STEG-oh-SORE-us**

Stygimoloch: **Stig-ee-MOE-lok**

Telmatosaurus: **tel-MA-toh-SORE-us**

Tenontosaurus: **ten-ON-toe-SORE-us**

Thalassodromeus: **thal-ahs-oh-DROH-mee-us**

Titanosaurus: **ti-TAN-oh-oh-SORE-us**

Tratayenia: **tra-ta-YEN-nee-ah**

Triceratops: **try-SEH-ra-tops**

Troodon: **TROH-oh-don**

Tupandactylus: **Too-pan-DACK-tih-lus**

Tyrannosaurus rex: **ty-RAN-oh-SORE-us REX**

Utahraptor: **YOO-tah-RAP-tor**

Velociraptor: **veh-LOSS-ee-rap-tuhr**

Wendiceratops: **when-di-SEH-ra-tops**

Yutyrannus: **uit-ty-RAN-us**

Zalmoxes: **zal-MOKS-eez**

Zuul: **zool**